wear your life well

HELENE OSEEN

wear your life well

praise

uplifting...intimate...encouraging...motivating...a must-read for all women.

"*Wear Your Life Well* is a quick read but one that will stay with you. I wouldn't classify this book as a traditional self-help book which I often find to be a bit overdone and tiresome. I was overcome with emotion while reading this wonderfully written book on life and style. It offers some beautiful advice for helping you accept, love, and just be yourself, and finding your beauty both on the inside and the outside, with words and stories that really grab and inspire you. It has beautiful moral lessons that are emotional, gripping and practical too.

This novel is a beautiful read and this is a book I know I will be coming back to again and again. It truly spoke to my heart. I sat the book down after finishing the last page, feeling so happy to be me, so excited for the future, and so grateful for the present."

MyStyleSpot
Amazon Top 100 Reviewer

"Helene understands the minds and hearts of women and speaks to us through her short, thought-provoking and change-creating stories. She has hacked life as a woman and shows us that a happier life can happen."

Michelle Cederberg
Health and Productivity Expert and author of *Energy Now! Small Steps to an Energetic Life.*

"Helene takes us on a journey of self-discovery in a book that you simply can't put down. Each story gave me the feeling that I was curled up on a couch with a wise friend, chatting over a glass of wine, sharing our thoughts and feelings, our celebrations and our challenges. We can all see ourselves in Helene's stories and while they are hers, they are ours too."

Jerilynn Daniels
Senior Manager, Community Investments & Marketing,
Public Affairs, Royal Bank of Canada.

"This highly personal, entertaining and touching book captures the warp and woof of the female experience. It is a tremendously inspiring and vitalizing read. Wherever you are on your life path, you'll find this book a perfect fit."

Flora Morris Brown
Life story facilitator and author of *Color your Life Happy: Create your unique path and Claim the Joy You Deserve.*

"A rare combination of honest, funny, poignant and enduring — an inspiring book worthy of the coveted night stand. Helene's writing style is inviting and conversational. This book is both beautiful and pragmatic. Bravo."

Jo Dibblee
Best-Selling author of *Frock Off: Living Undisguised.*

"I don't typically read personal development books, but this book is different. Helene doesn't pretend to have the answers to life — she simply shares her journey in a way that illuminates and helps me to understand mine (and makes me feel good about myself). I love this book."

Leslie Gell
Realtor ® Royal LePage Benchmark.

"Helene writes from her heart and her warmth and deep conviction shine through on every page. There are so many gems of wisdom, inspiration and practical advice that my copy is filled with page markers and sticky notes."

Vikki MacKinnon
Master Numerologist and author of *Please Take a Number.*

"Reading *Wear Your Life Well* is like slipping on your favorite sweater. By encouraging us to think bigger, laugh louder and be bolder, Helene has given us a gift and wrapped it with style."

Dr. Trina Read
Best-Selling author of *Till Sex Do Us Part.*

"Helene Oseen will help you clean out the closets of your life. *Wear Your Life Well* is a woman's manifesto for empowerment and self-acceptance. In her heart-warming book, Helene explores women's closets literally and as a life metaphor with elegance and openness."

Patricia Morgan
Therapist and author of *From woe to WOW: How Resilient Women Succeed at Work.*

"*Wear Your Life Well* is a powerful book that prompts you to ask yourself life-changing questions. It made me stop and ponder my life — my past, present and my future. There are so many truths that Helene writes about and so many fears that each of us face daily, I realized I am not alone in many of the issues that so many women battle through their adult years."

Shannon Sambells
Mystic and author of *To Touch the Hand of God.*

Wear Your Life Well: Lessons on the Journey to your Truest Self is filled with relatable insights and wisdom, generously sprinkled with profound thoughts, and blended with just the right amount of humor and reality. Once I started reading it, I didn't want to stop."

Iris Talbot
Voice Coach for Singers and Speakers.

copyright

Publisher

HOP
CALGARY

ISBN 978-0-9682585-1-4

ISBN 978-0-9682585-2-1 (ebook)

This book is available at special discounts when purchased in bulk for premium and sales promotions as well as for fund-raising use.

Design by Jacquie Morris
Artwork Image #848878 Dodeskaden/iStockPhoto

Printed in Canada

FIRST EDITION

wear your life well

für elise

my mother. my friend.

Experience is the hardest kind of teacher. It gives you the test first and the lesson afterward.

~Oscar Wilde

contents

foreword by *Catherine Ford*   15

woman to woman   21

design *your* life

get into change shape   25

express your essence   29

find your groove   31

decide your destiny   33

start where you are   37

believe that good things are on their way   41

forget about being perfect   45

mind your thoughts   51

believe in day dreams   53

knock on the door   57

do it for you   61

say YES to being a rock star   65

reinvent yourself   69

find joy on the journey   73

fashion *your* style

make room for a new you   79

recognize your value   83

claim your confidence   85

stay true to yourself   87

learn to say NO   93

reveal your true colors   95

live a colorful life   97

walk on the wild side   101

love what you've got   103

treat yourself gently   107

don't label yourself   109

search for something new   111

uncover your secret strength   115

know you are deserving   117

love *your* life

forgive yourself   123

find your voice   127

make a difference   131

cherish your mother   135

embrace your evolution   139

get playful   143

find your funny   145

get over getting older   147

be your own hero   151

grow through life   153

never give up   155

look for the treasures in life's scars   161

live like there's no tomorrow   163

share your story   167

off the cuff   171

my manifesto   173

acknowledgments   175

about the author   177

life makeover   181

wear your life well

foreword

It takes courage to tell the truth about your life to a friend; it takes a special kind of courage to tell the world. Luckily, Helene Oseen has a healthy dose of that necessary moral, emotional and practical grit.

She also apparently didn't get the message promoted by fashion nay-sayers who insist women's clothes — combined with the adornments we put on our bodies, from shoes to hair clips — are not important. That what we wear and the art of storytelling aren't soul mates. Helene knows, as do most of the iconic fashion designers, that it is storytelling that fuels creativity, regardless of the method or material.

That she didn't get the message is good, because Helene combines form and function, style and substance so perfectly in *Wear Your Life Well*. That metaphorical title is a lot more literal than figurative.

Full disclosure: Helene has been a friend of mine for more than 20 years. She is my go-to style guru and sometimes my sounding board, although my taste (what there is of it) in clothes will occasionally bring a mild rebuke from her. She didn't volunteer advice, I elicited this commentary by asking for her approval. She once explained in exquisite detail why an outfit I lusted for would definitely be all wrong for me, my body shape and my fashion "personality." The fact I listened to her is testament to her eye for what is both stylish and appropriate. Okay, this did not quench my lust for this particular outfit, but of course I did not buy it. (There are moments when I see someone 30 years younger, 20 pounds lighter and 10 inches taller in the mirror.) Because I'm a woman, sometimes the obverse is true. Don't we all own those "fat" clothes for when we're feeling frumpy? Helene knows all about those days.

Every woman needs a friend like Helene, one who can look you in the eye and tell you the truth. Yes, those pants do make your ass look fat. Well, Helene is always far more polite than that, but you get the message. In her book, you get the Helene I know and that's just perfect.

We have laughed and cried together, shared stories, food and wine, walked and talked and talked and talked. And to quote Dorothy Parker from her 1944 book *The Standard of Living*: "Constant use had not worn ragged the fabric of their friendship."

But there are stories in this book I never knew; depths of truth that would be impossible except in the written word. The book is dedicated to her mother, Elise, and it is obvious Helene learned the lessons of love and privation; hardships and triumphs; discrimination and strength from Elise. There are lessons most of us daughters hear from our mothers. These are the stories that have shaped the women we became, the choices we made and the truths that are, in essence, universal. All women share in them.

There are stories here that will bring a tear to your eye and ones that will make you laugh out loud. Who could not laugh at being asked if one wanted the seniors' discount? Helene's ability to tell the truth serves her well. She lets us in on her personal journey — warts and all, so to speak. She talks about self-doubt and success, about failure and love and how all of that molds us into the strong and resilient women we should all be.

All women know about how clothing makes us feel and Helene shares the stories of her mother making her clothes and the familiar sounds of the sewing machine and the lessons in how to choose fabric. In that, Helene and I share more than a common growing-up experience. I never thought the clothes my mother made for me were homemade because we could not afford store-bought; instead they were special. My mother, Margaret Ford, taught herself how to knit and promptly fashioned three matching Siwash sweaters — complete with multi-hued mallards on the back — one for my father, Bob, and one each for her daughters. I don't believe she ever saw a genuine Cowichan knitted sweater, but that was irrelevant, even though that's what they were — as fashioned by an Irish war bride who had never felt the true cold of a winter until she arrived in Canada with me in tow. I remember how warm those sweaters were in a cold Edmonton winter.

(Mother was very good at learning by doing, learning by watching — not for her the slow process of taking a class. She'd wait until one of her friends did a course and then demand to watch the process. She would tackle anything that needed doing, from carpentry to cement mixing. In the process, she laid her own patio. If you could read directions — oh, hell, even if there were no directions or she ignored them — Mother believed no do-it-yourself project was impossible. She once took out the kitchen breakfast nook with an axe and a crowbar after bruising her hip for the umpteenth time.)

But her true creativity came at her sewing machine. I still remember fondly the pinstriped gabardine suit, lined in red satin, Mother made for me when I was in university in Edmonton. It was fashioned from an old suit of my father's.

Later, when I was living in London, Ont. and had to take one of my suits to a tailor, he wanted to know who had made it.

I asked "why?"

"Because I'd like to hire him," was the reply.

I laughed out loud and said I didn't think my mother was looking for work. Besides, she was living in Red Deer, Alberta.

When my sister was married, the only purchased outfit was a new suit for Dad. The bride made her own dress, as did the mother of the bride. As for the maid of honor — me, the older sister — her dress was handmade in absentia (I was living in Toronto at the time) and perfectly matched the ribbon trimming the bride's gown. Such memories of "things" are more than just the rags and remnants of memory — they are part of the fabric of our lives.

So when men ask why (with a very tired tone of voice) we "need" another pair of black slacks or a thousand pairs of shoes, we know the secret behind those closet shelves: any of us who battle with our weight and self-image know that shoes can comfort us. With only a few exceptions, they always fit. They can make us feel sexy or businesslike or both in some cases. They can be an expression of our inner self. They can also be a balm when nothing in the closet fits except for a special pair of shoes. Long years ago, shortly after I met my now-husband, he was in Holt Renfrew in Calgary with me. A testament to new love is that fact: he was in a clothing store with me. Not only that, he sat still while I tried on shoes. (There's a reason smart women's stores supply comfortable and convenient places for menfolk to sit: keep them happy when they don't really want to be there.)

I tried on a pair of "granny" boots that felt like I was wearing kid leather gloves on my feet. I've never had trouble with shoes and the fit, or the heel height for that matter, but these were

18

something special. Alas, they were $315, a price so outrageous to me at the time that I balked at spending that much on a single pair of shoes. Then I looked at Ted and noticed a thin line of sweat forming on his upper lip. (At least I thought that and it makes a good story.) I bought the boots immediately and wore them for years. They continued to give me pleasure every time I wore them.

That one pair of treasured boots lasted long years after we had been married, long years after I realized Ted loathed all forms of shopping except for food, particularly cheese, and especially if the shopping entailed a trip to any farmers' market.

By now you've noticed my own reminisces, all brought forward in my memory by reading *Wear Your Life Well*. I hope you, too, by reading Helene's stories can call up those special moments in your life that bring you love, hope and joy.

Catherine Ford

wear your life well

woman to woman

My life is my message.

~Mahatma Ghandi

I love the company of women. I realized how important we are to each other early in life and over the years have come to appreciate the bonds that connect us from childhood to old age. Many of us share a culture or special rituals with each other while we fashion intimacy through conversations and clothes. Often those conversations are prompted by our clothes.

We share secrets, tell each other stories, and give each other advice. We kvetch, we laugh and we console each other. It's through such honest and vulnerable moments that we fashion strong connections. We discover we are not alone. We talk about life and how to get through crises as well as where we bought those fabulous boots. Sometimes all in the same sentence. Let's face it, we like our clothes, shoes and shopping. I'm not saying that we live our life as a fashion statement but then again, we connect immediately when we gush over each other's outfits because it's a subtle way of saying I see you, I like you, and we can be friends.

Everyone has a story. Everyone has a struggle. Our stories are the fabric of our lives. Sometimes we wear burlap. Sometimes we wear silk. Stories are the seams that connect us as we sew together our shared experiences. Our victories. Our fears. Our deepest concerns.

We see life through the prism of story. We each write our own and it's an exercise in not only looking in the mirror but also looking deep down into our hearts and souls. We are not one story. We can change our story — and everyone needs help and encouragement along the way.

My story is about change and transition. It's about deciding my life is my own. It's the slice-of-life stuff that we all experience on our journey to express our essence and to stay true to ourselves.

What dreams do you have tucked away? My aim is to help you awaken your inner voice and say *yes* to your reinvention destination even if it feels selfish or scary. I would be breaking a girlfriend code if we didn't talk about clothes too, so I'll help you pick out something to wear for those day-to-day occasions that stand for your life.

I share my journey through intimate stories, reflections, anecdotes and musings. I divulge the challenges and lessons that have made the greatest differences in my life. I am not here to tell you what to do but only to tell you my secrets and stories so that hopefully you can glean something useful.

You can live by design, rather than by default. Life on your terms doesn't require drastic measures — although it could. Be it a major move, a minor tweak, or a new look, I'll prompt you to think about your wishes and hopes and then encourage you to give yourself permission to be daring, bold and true to yourself. If you don't fit your life, change your life to fit you.

The world is your runway.

wear your life well

get into change shape

It takes courage to stay interested — to be interesting — and to live an interesting life. You have to reinvent yourself over and over.

~Robin Fisher Roffer

Ever wondered *what's next*?

I have learned that just when I think everything in my life is under control, suddenly it's not. Bam. Everything changes. Guaranteed.

An unexpected event occurs. The need for change is black and white. And, from time to time even when my life is status quo, I ponder the shades of grey, like why – when nothing is really wrong — I start to experience a shift, a restlessness an understanding that I am starting to get stir-crazy with certain aspects. There is a little voice nagging me to make some changes but I'm not exactly sure what those changes would look like. I have learned over time that those little things nag at me for a reason; so now I give them a voice and a place in my life.

Steve Jobs once shared that he would look in the mirror every day and ask himself "If today were the last day of my life, would I want to do what I am about to do?" He believed that when the answer was NO for too many days he knew he needed to change something.

I like that.

Transformation doesn't come easily because it's human nature for us to resist change. Whether we want or need to change, shift is a constant in our lives that, quite frankly, we don't know how to handle well. There is no how-to manual, a one-size-fits-all solution, because transition is a personal experience for each of us. Ultimately change brings us closer to who we are as we embrace and expand our own humanity.

Reinvention is not a re-do because we didn't do something right the first time. It's an opportunity to consciously redesign any part of our life — a little bit at a time — by building on all that we have accomplished and the lessons we have learned as we chart our unique journey toward success and satisfaction. It makes no difference whether we are seeking a personal or a professional tweak; it's an on-going evolution that makes us feel like a new person and yet more like ourselves than ever before.

Every so often the very thought of switching things up terrifies me — almost to the point of immobilizing me. Welcome or not, change always takes some getting used to. So I resolve that no matter how daunting, difficult or frightening it may be, I can do it if I take it one step at a time. That helps me to push past my angst and helps me to obliterate that feeling of being utterly and uncontrollably overwhelmed during the shake-up.

I have discovered that the journey to change involves several steps. Sometimes they play out in slow motion and in other situations they need to be dealt with in fast-forward mode because they are so instant and urgent.

Here's how I get ready to take a leap and make it an exciting and energizing adventure to a new beginning and something great.

Reflect

Knowing what I want makes the process easier but sometimes I just don't know — yet. So I start the search for answers. Clearing my mind gives me energy and allows me to focus on the path ahead as I take the time to think about the big things in my life and to reflect consciously on what really matters to me. I punctuate my thoughts with more question marks than periods.

Those who know me will agree that patience is not one of my strong virtues. *I want to know, and I want to know now* could easily be a mantra for me. Yet, I have learned to be okay with myself while I am in the thinking stage and to understand that I shouldn't make the mistake of rushing into the doing stage.

Renew

As I begin the journey to the person I truly want to be I make commitments to myself that I will keep. No empty promises. By making my dreams a size too big I can grow into them. Once I have a clear vision I start basing my decisions on things that will make me happier and move me toward my destination. I want to feel my passion and I want to be clear about what makes me want to get out of bed in the morning as I reclaim my personal power and acknowledge what is right with my life and let go of what isn't.

Relax

Change always takes much longer than I expect. I accept that it's all right to not know the answers. They will come when I least expect them. I give myself permission to explore and embrace what's next. I try to be gentle with myself, to let go of fear of failure. I don't let myself get caught up in perfection paralysis.

I know that reinvention never stops. Transformation is a choice I make moment by moment each and every day. I know that my happiness is not a dot at the end of a road — a final destination — instead it comes from the many places where I can grow as I experience my experiences and feel my feelings. Sometimes change is magnificent and exhilarating. Other times it's messy and painful. Either way I can't hold back change. I can choose how I react to it and ensure that it serves to inspire me — not terrify me.

At the end of it all, I hope I can say that I have become a more courageous and graceful self and that I've lived the full length and width of my life.

We are all frightened by change and the unfamiliar, but those who remain receptive — despite their reluctances — can discover new passions and possibilities.

How can you make your life more awesome than it is now? I challenge you to imagine your next steps using your own uniqueness, to get out of your comfort zone and to feel excited about a future full of possibility. Then take a bold step forward because it's up to you to put new life into the life you've been living.

You must make the choice to take a chance if you want anything in your life to change. Every chapter of your life demands a different you. Embrace change, harness its power and realize your dreams.

express your essence

Today you are you that is truer than true. There is no one alive who is Youer than YOU.

~Dr. Seuss

Who are YOU? It's THE essential question.

I'm not asking about what you do. You are more than the roles you play every day. If you had to tell me about yourself without talking about your job or your family what would you say? Can you shed the layers?

Who are you at your core?

Answering this question is the work of life; the work of soul. We are not who we were yesterday or will be tomorrow. Think about it. It's crazy how we can look back just a year and see how much has changed. People have come into our lives – others have left. We have created memories to cherish and have lived through moments we wish we could forget. There are subtle connections between our past and our future that are intricately intertwined. Our experiences and relationships help us to make meaning of our thoughts, behaviors and feelings as we authenticate our values. Sometimes it takes a sudden change to initiate the on-going, soul-searching understanding of self. Other times, it's a more gradual process. We have choices about change. We can decide what we want — and don't want — going forward.

Just because something once was, doesn't mean it still has to be. It is also true that we can choose to have even more of something that already makes us happy. And we can even manifest things we want into our lives that haven't shown up yet.

Reinvention is simply becoming more of who you are. We can react and even plan with confidence knowing that we have everything we need right inside us to create the life we deserve.

What do you want in your life?

Listen to your heart. Go inside. Go deep down. Ask yourself those sometimes-uncomfortable questions. Don't limit yourself by should have — could have — would have. You still can. Decide your life right now.

As I have travelled the roads of my life I have always known that I will never really arrive or even fully understand the destination. I take heart in appreciating that no matter what I am doing, or where I find myself, I can journey in the right direction. And you can too.

find your groove

The two most important days in your life are the day you are born and the day you find out why.

~Mark Twain

I have been immersed in fashion and style my entire life, going back to childhood. My mother was a recent immigrant to Canada and a young widow. Like so many European women in the early 1950s she was a seamstress. To satisfy both her creativity and the need to provide for her family she sewed for her clientele and for me. I remember the sound of her Singer sewing machine lulling me to sleep at night. Sometimes I would wake up and there would be clothes for me. I didn't have a lot of clothes but they were impeccable, custom-made, and they made me feel good. My mother instilled in me early the importance of appreciating what is fine in life and cultivating a sense of *style*.

There were no fashion magazines in our house. The tight budget didn't allow for them. On a Saturday afternoon you would often find me and mom at the fabric store. It was our own special time together. We would pour over pattern books and assess the potential of various bolts of material. By the time I was 10 I had a tireless curiosity about what could be done with fabric, color, texture and design. I loved all the factors that went into making the choices and I began to understand how dressing is one of the most creative and expressive outlets available to all of us. I loved playing dress-up.

Consequently, I never really understood just how unnerving fashion and style could be to so many people. I always had an eye

— a level of esthetic savvy — and people often asked my advice to help them pick out the right clothing for them. I came to understand that clothes can make women feel better about themselves.

My interest in fashion grew into a passion, and that helped me to understand my gift and how to use it in a meaningful way.

After all, what is life without a sense of purpose. Therefore, I postulate that our purpose is to live our life to the truest and fullest expression of who we are by exploring and integrating our divergent, interesting and eclectic aspects. It's easy to get stuck spending too much time looking for the bliss in the BIG dream instead of savouring the smaller steps, the in-between, and saying YES to the threads that stitch our life together.

In other words, I have come to understand that if you do what you love, and love what you do, you will feel light-hearted for no apparent reason. And when life wreaks mayhem, you will stay inspired to keep pushing through the turmoil, disappointments and challenges that are inevitable.

decide your destiny

You have brains in your head and feet in your shoes, you can steer yourself in any direction you choose. You're on your own and you know what you know, and you are the one who'll decide where to go.

~Dr. Seuss

Back in 1987 I was at the local Superstore and passed by a display of books on my way to the grocery section. *Fashion Formula* by Mary Duffy seemed to jump off the shelf at me as though it had a message. I got excited just reading the title. I'd never come across a book like it before — a book devoted to helping you understand your body type and how to dress to accentuate your positives while taking into consideration coloring, lifestyle and personality.

What fun, I thought. Could I actually get paid to help women with this?

In the 1980s image consulting was a fledgling industry in the U.S. and almost unheard of in Canada. I knew if I was going to do this professionally I wanted and needed more depth than just reading a book and trusting my instincts.

At that time, I was working as co-ordinator for the *Further Education Council.* I had no idea how to make this career transition happen. I felt trapped in an abusive marriage and I knew my controlling husband would be angry. He wanted a doormat and a trophy wife. I yearned for respect for my abilities and worth as a woman.

I wanted it enough to figure out a way to get it. And I did. We were wealthy, but he made sure I knew that it was "his money" and he wanted no part of financing my foolishness. Even though I had my own employment income the bank would not issue a credit card or offer a loan without my husband's signatory consent. This remained a remnant of how women were treated when they were deemed possessions of their husbands.

The stand-off was gruelling but I was relentless in my asking and eventually he agreed reluctantly to co-sign a loan for me thinking that a new "hobby" would keep his little woman happy.

I got my certification as an Image Consultant at Fashion Academy in Los Angeles. Step by step I started to uncover and recover my strength. I started consulting which provided me with a sense of purpose but an inconsistent income. I was scared but I ended my marriage, moved out of my luxury home, rented a small apartment and took control of my life. I didn't have the self-esteem or energy to fight for myself and my worth so I walked away with nothing — but my dignity, my children and a hope for a better life.

I needed a steady income. Even though I had no retail experience the first job I was offered was as store manager for a fashion chain. It turned out to be anything but my dream job — as a matter of fact I didn't like it at all. I was offended by the culture. We had a fundamental difference in our philosophy of how to motivate and treat employees to produce results. The chain wanted a tyrant who was willing to treat the staff without respect and even bully them if it meant getting the sales figures up. I wanted to empower and teach my staff the fundamentals of fashion and how to build a loyal clientele — a person who feels appreciated will always do more than expected.

They told me that retail staff was too transitory for that type of investment. I told them if we invested in them they wouldn't be so transitory.

They told me I was fired.

As a single mother of two my life was filled with financial stress. It wasn't long before a new opportunity presented itself to me when a high-end Edmonton store expanded to Calgary. I was hired as their Image Consultant. This position was already in place in luxury, brand and designer stores in New York but was a new and unproven concept in Calgary, Canada.

I recall vividly the Grand Opening. The store was so busy that there were long line-ups for the fitting rooms as women with arms full of expensive garments awaited their turn to try them on. One woman who selected her own garments stepped out of the fitting room and prompted me for a response as she gushed "I look *so* fantastic — do *you* think so too?"

The "look" was slightly less than amazing; actually, it was horrible on her. Everything about it was wrong. I tried to measure my response so as not to insult her and at the same time offer some much-needed expertise. "We can do better. Let me find something else for you." Her face was beaming as she declared. "You pass! I'll work with you."

She was the first long-term client I cultivated; hundreds and hundreds more would become my clients over the years. My business built through word-of-mouth and soon women came from across the country to shop with me. We would work several hours at a time and always by appointment. They didn't seem to mind booking well in advance in order to ensure they would get my advice before they would spend thousands of dollars on new clothes.

I learned a lot about women on the other side of the dressing room door. I heard their stories. Some had major shifts and changes in their lives, some positive, some negative. Sometimes my clients thought they were just shopping for some new clothes — in fact after hearing their stories, I knew they were shopping for a whole new life. I came to know that when we change on the inside it's only natural that we want to look new on the outside too. The clothes we wear are just an extension of who we are — they are tied to our self-identity and we outgrow who we are in the transition from one phase of our life to another.

Sometimes a little retail therapy is easier than asking the hard questions about life.

The answer is *never* in a shopping bag.

start where you are

It isn't where you came from; it's where you're going that counts

~Ella Fitzgerald

I was never a career fashionista with a closet full of clothes and credit card debt to match. I needed a more sensible approach to dressing in my life. A client once told me she kept her credit card balances to the maximum for security reasons — just in case anyone ever stole them. That always made me smile.

It was a struggle being a single mom and raising two children on a retail salary. I was Image Consultant in a high-end store by day and cleaning lady in that same store every Sunday night. I was okay with that because I know there is dignity in work. I did it to survive.

I vividly remember the day I was working with one of my regular clients; she was a professional woman who flew across the country twice a year to shop with me. I spent several hours with her at each visit and she would walk out of the store having spent about $2500. That was a lot of money in the early 1990s.

After her session I was exhausted, happy and hungry. I went to the bank machine to withdraw $20 and the message that funds were not available devastated me. I didn't have enough money to buy lunch. It was a moment that changed the course of my life. Right then and there I found the resolve and the courage to step up to my potential.

But where to start?

In my head, I decided. I asked myself three basic questions. What do I want? What do I have? What do I need?

I knew I wanted more. I wanted to thrive. That meant taking it to the next level, spinning it around, turning it upside down and being brave enough to be bold. I wasn't sure what *it* was but as I came up with ideas things began to evolve. If I was going to move my life forward and make my life better, it was up to me to take a chance and do things differently.

I understood that in order to attract opportunity I needed to look at where I was, work hard, take risks and take control of my destiny.

When I was a girl I wanted to be a teacher, but given our circumstances a university education wasn't possible. It was an empowering moment for me when I realized that I could still teach — not children in a classroom, but adults.

I was aware that I had a natural gift as a communicator. I took some classes and honed and polished my skill set. I started hosting in-store seminars for customers, soon companies were hiring me for conferences and then I started doing one-day seminars for the School of Management at the University of Calgary. I was proud of myself. Throughout my life I had often felt *less than* or ashamed because I had never attended university. Now I was teaching in one on a regular basis. From there I developed and for a number of years taught an 80-hour Certificate Program for Retail Fashion Consultants at the Southern Alberta Institute of Technology (now SAIT Polytechnic).

Doors were starting to open everywhere.

A fashion/lifestyle journalist at the *Calgary Herald* quoted me in her articles and stories. That helped my visibility and established my expertise to a broader audience. As a result, I was offered the opportunity to write a weekly column for that same newspaper and *Fashion 911®* was launched. I was an expert but not a journalist and sometimes I felt like an interloper. Then one day my editor asked me to write occasional full-page lifestyle features. It was then that I accepted this truth — that others believed in my ability more than I did. I worked hard to prove them right. Simultaneously, during that same six-year time period, I appeared on weekly *Fashion 911®* television segments for the local Saturday Morning Breakfast Show.

When I decided to "take a chance" on me, I was still working in retail full-time. My moonlighting career took me places I never thought I would go — ultimately to being the boss of me.

Look at the opportunity around you. Take it.

It's yours.

wear your life well

believe that good things are on their way

My life ... is about not knowing, having to change, taking the moment and making the best of it, without knowing what's going to happen next.

~Gilda Radner

You never, ever know when something that changes your life is about to happen. We don't get to see what comes next.

A prominent oil company executive sought me out by asking around about who would be the best person to help solve his dilemma. My name kept coming up. We met and I was ecstatic about the new opportunity he presented. I became the Managing Partner of an independent boutique in one of the most affluent sections of the city just steps away from the Calgary Golf and Country Club. He had deep pockets and I had the know-how.

The backstory: This man had purchased the business for his new, much younger, wife because she loved to play dress-up. The previous owner had built a highly-profitable business with a loyal clientele. She was ready to retire and sold him the business. Properly managed it could have been a turn-key operation.

But it takes more than a love of fashion to run a business. You need a plan, skill and commitment. The wife had none of these attributes and quickly ran the business into the red. She rarely came into the store and the only thing that intrigued her was the buying trips to New York. She had no understanding of what she was doing and filled her store with expensive designer, Barbie-type clothing that was perfect for the glamourous ladies who lunch. Women just like her. The traditional clientele comprised successful, executive, and well-to-do middle-aged women. Under new management they couldn't find clothing that fit their image anymore. So, they took their business elsewhere.

Over the next several years I turned the store around and it was once again a highly-respected shopping destination for women who wanted both fashion advice and stylish clothing that fit their lifestyle. As the fashion buyer, I made sure the "right" clothing was hanging on the racks. The former clients came back and new customers flooded in. Even in the day-to-day my career was a perfect fit and I was having a ton of fun. Unbeknownst to me an unexpected change was about to strike lightning fast and send me into a nose-dive.

I remember all too clearly the moment it happened.

During what I thought was going to be a run-of-the-mill meeting, my partner announced that his marriage was over. He had decided to close the store because he didn't want to be reminded of her in any way. The store no longer had purpose in his life.

I probably went through three stages of grief simultaneously as I tried to make sense of what had just happened. At first, I was numb, which probably allowed me to survive emotionally. Then came the denial. Some moments all I could hear in my head was "No! This can't be real." I felt gutted. I reassured myself that I could move past my grief, face it and survive. I told myself "things will work out," just as they always have if I trust myself to life. But, deep inside I just wasn't buying the goods I was trying to sell myself.

I cried a lot. I was confused, angry and anxious.

Being the extrovert I am, it made no sense to me or anyone else that I just wanted to withdraw, to disengage from my friends and many of the things I used to enjoy doing. But that is what I did. I knew that I had to take alone time to allow my heart to heal so it could tell me what it truly wanted. I did a lot of digging in the dirt as I tended my garden and my soul. I had two choices: to panic or to take action.

I was able to come to terms with my loss as I moved into the acceptance phase with a resounding "Yes! It happened."

Life isn't fair – *so what*.

I needed money. I needed it fast. I answered a job posting for a Business and Communications Program Designer for the Board of Education in their Continuing Education Department. It was the type of work I was doing before my foray into the fashion world and it made sense for me to revisit it now that the store had closed.

I got the job. The position was part-time, just four days a week. That meant I could keep a roof over my head and still have enough time to have a moonlighting career pursuing my fashion passion. I was doing interesting work that mattered -- helping others (as well as myself) continue the life-long journey of learning.

I started to find some calm in the chaos, accepting the new normal and affirming the plot twist. Realizing that I had the strength to evolve life's not-so-fun surprise into a bold new chapter of my life was empowering. By simply re-framing my reference I could approach this change as an adventure. I needed to go through what I was going through and when I did my energy level came back and so did my love of life. The storm had passed and the sun shone again. But it wasn't until I started looking for the colors in the rainbow that I found gold in the stunning new place I found myself.

Life isn't a dress rehearsal so we must go after what we want. And sometimes despite a lot of hard work and dedication, we might not always get what we think we deserve.

It doesn't matter.

What does matter is what people think about us when they hear our name. That is something that we can control — the reputation we have and the relationships we've developed. That is what will open doors.

I was propelled forward by people who believed in me and I went places that I never imagined.

So, thank you, change.

forget about being perfect

Yes, I am imperfect and vulnerable and sometimes afraid, but that doesn't change the truth that I am also brave and worthy of love and belonging.

~Brené Brown – *The Gifts of Imperfection*

Scottie said he fell in love with me partly because during our first lunch together my jacket collar was turned up the whole time and I didn't even know it. That imperfection cinched it. I had been playing telephone tag with one of my clients, an executive recruiter. She had an interest in fashion and also thought that taking one of my classes would benefit the work she did with leaders. In my initial message to her that morning I mentioned my *Fashion 911®* column in the *Calgary Herald* that day because it was certainly not one of my usual topics. She had asked Scottie, a management consultant in their small office, not to put me on hold or take a message if I called when she was on the other line. She wanted to make sure she could talk to me directly and he was to keep me engaged.

That's exactly how it played out. We were able to make small talk because, with a touch of serendipity, he had just read my column. I went on to tell him what an interesting day I was having because of an angry phone call. In the end, he made me laugh about the whole thing. I thought he was pretty funny. I had no idea if he was married or single, young or old. I wasn't looking for a date. He was just a guy who seemed to be one of the nice people in the world.

Earlier that morning, an upset paramedic had called me in a rage, yelling at me for being blasphemous to the honor of first responders, trivializing the good work they do by attaching 911 to the word *fashion*. I actually held the phone away from my ear until he stopped screaming. He wasn't one of the nice people.

Coincidence (or not) the column published that very day was in response to another angry male. And that was the basis of my first exchange with Scottie.

FASHION   CALGARY HERALD

Tuesday, October 22, 1996

'Image' said unrelated to job performance

Dear Helene,

I read with great interest, your response to the long-term employee (Joan) concerning the meaning of 'casual day' in the workplace. You seem to imply that we should fear for our jobs if we don't dress in a certain way. You even mentioned a scientific connection between image and financial success.

Apparently you consider it perfectly acceptable for someone's work to be rejected because of their 'image.' I see this as prejudice and bigotry, plain and simple. No study in the world can prove the guy wearing the suit does a better job than the guy wearing jeans and a tee-shirt when doing the same task.

What matters is your work ethic and the ability to do the job at hand. If your clients are basing their judgments on anything else BUT good honest hard work, they aren't doing their jobs properly.

Rejection on the basis of 'image' is dangerous because ideals of racism and homophobia can easily be masked.

I dislike suits. They are ugly, uncomfortable, expensive to buy and even more expensive to keep clean. Why should I have to wear one? I don't expect anyone else to. It should be a personal choice. Isn't that one of the benefits of democracy?

Remember, racists are also more interested in image than ability and supposedly have scientific studies to show the connections between their ideas of image and success. In my view, your attitude is not different.

Michael

Dear Michael,

You are right, Michael — looking good does not influence your ability to do your job. However, once again, I will reinforce my position that a person's perception is in fact their reality. I did not say we live in a perfect world.

Democracy works for everyone or it isn't a democracy. The issue really boils down to company image. The person who hires you has a right to expect you to present a positive image of the company in all you do. They may feel that careless attention to one's self-image may extend a carelessness in the workplace. You can choose your attire if you are self-employed. If you are working for someone I am sure you will agree they should have an equal opportunity of choosing whom they want to work for them. A reasonable commitment to the image they want their company to portray may be part of the job requirements.

You mention the 'benefits of democracy.' That extends to both employer as well as employee. People doing business with you or hiring you can choose not to employ you or do business with you if they don't like the 'cut of your cloth.' That is why I suggested people need to clarify what is considered reasonable wearing apparel in their place of employment.

Helene

Scottie read my column that day and saw my picture. It was his background check on me. He's not the kind of guy who reads fashion. He's Eddie Bauer all the way. His response to our phone conversation was a note:

Helene,

You have indeed accomplished something in that I have never before sought out the fashion section of the newspaper. On the other hand, I have never been acquainted with (if 20 seconds on the phone is an acquaintance) a racist, homophobic, old-lady-hating, paramedic abusing fashion writer. Who would have thought the fashion section is more fun than Oprah or the comics?

It really was a good response. I get the sense that no matter how logical you may be, or how accurate your observation of human nature, the letter writer won't get it. I often feel sorry for those who can't understand that no matter how comfortable sweats may be, they don't open doors. I may be biased as I think suits are both comfortable and look good. Does this make me racist and homophobic as well? I wonder.

Here's a coincidence I hope you appreciate. After our quick phone conversation both you and I said to Kendra "I would like to meet him/her." She had a good laugh at that. She speaks extremely highly of you and she and I agree on most people which might just mean we are both really warped. The meandering point of this paragraph is to see if you would really like to meet. Coffee, lunch, dinner or a walk next week sometime would be great. Vegas would be fun but next week is a little busy. Please let me know.

Hope to hear from you soon.

Scottie

Sometimes, you really do just know. We met for lunch a few days later. Within the week we both recognized it was going to be forever. That was 20 years ago. Since then he has seen a lot more of my imperfections and quirks. He loves me not in spite of them, but because of them, and when things don't go exactly as I had hoped he opts to love me even more.

I'm a recovering perfectionist. My happiness doesn't mean that everything is perfect, it means that I have decided to look past my imperfections and allow gifts into my life.

Anna Quidlen once said "The thing that is really hard, and really amazing is giving up on being perfect and beginning the work of becoming yourself."

I agree.

I now know that I was born to be real, not perfect.

And, Scottie doesn't let me forget that I am the perfect woman for him.

wear your life well

mind your thoughts

You've been criticizing yourself for years and it hasn't worked.
Try approving of yourself and see what happens.

~Louise Hay

Every now and then I hear a voice. It's insidious. It's mean. I'm sure that a shrink would have a fancy-schmancy name for it but, in fact, I am aware that the voice is my own — it lives inside my head. From time to time I suffer from what I refer to as NGE Syndrome. That's when I think I am Not Good Enough.

Sometimes I say things to myself that I would never even consider saying to someone I dislike. That voice nags me and would have me believe that I'm inadequate, not good enough, not deserving.

When my other voice interrupts, it tells me that I am a good and loving person who works hard and who deserves to have a great life. Deep in my heart I know that voice is right. I'm a glass-half-full kind of gal, yet, sometimes getting that nasty voice to shut up and go away isn't easy.

So how do I get out of the funk without freaking out? I *choose* not to believe the bad things I tell myself.

Confidence is a state of mind. Confidence has nothing to do with how the outside world sees us. We believe erroneously that our value is somehow directly connected with what we do, our relationships, how much money we have, our appearance or any other external factor. In fact, confidence is rooted in our own perception of ourselves. It is not until we make peace with ourselves that goodness flows into our lives. For many years one

51

of my affirmations has been "I am imperfect and I am enough." When I am self-doubting I repeat this mantra that I have come to know from Brené Brown, not personally but from her book *The Gifts of Imperfection*. The irony is that being comfortable with a perceived lack is a catalyst to give myself permission to accept myself more fully.

I have stopped obsessing about becoming a more perfect version of me. I know that no amount of self-improvement can replace self-acceptance. When I am gentle, kind and loving with myself I am able to focus on my true source of happiness — my growth and well-being.

Be your own best friend.

believe in day dreams

Even the wildest dreams have to start somewhere. Allow yourself the time and space to let your mind wander and imagination fly.

~Oprah Winfrey

Many say that meditation can bring profound depth and insight into our lives. So, in order to hear my inner voice, I tried. I failed. I can't keep my mind still. It's a painful process for me. I can't seem to quiet my mind on demand as I think about not thinking.

Often my mind races, as does my mouth. At those times Scottie reminds me that it would be nice to have some kind of transition statement before I changed topics so that he can open the appropriate file folder in his brain to keep up with the conversation.

So you can imagine why, when he walked into the room and found me sitting on the couch, spaced out and staring out the window, he asked me if everything was all right. It was. He also wondered what I was thinking about.

Hmm...good questions.

Perhaps my brain was wandering simply because it could during a rather mundane day at the end of a week of down time. Truthfully, I was bored so instead of turning on the television or reading another book I chose to stay inside my head instead. My thoughts were unintended and unrelated to anything and mostly flitted from one thing to the next which is out of character for me. Most of the time my mind is engaged in goal-directed thought. This time I wasn't analyzing, strategizing, setting goals, or figuring out my feelings; my mind was completely relaxed.

When my daughter was in grade school I was once told at a Parent/Teacher interview that she was a good student but that I should discourage her from daydreaming. It was seen as a behavioral disorder; that she might become too absorbed in her own world and out of touch with reality.

Nonsense.

While daydreaming is often seen as a lazy, non-productive pastime, there are many examples in recent studies of how it enhances creativity and improves thinking. Nowadays it is understood that it has the same affect as meditation, visualization or guided imagery, which are not only socially acceptable but also encouraged in the pursuit of success.

Your daydreams hold the answers. I know when I am daydreaming my brain is mulling over, processing and making sense of things in my life at a sub-conscious level. I am not even aware of what is going on as random thoughts, images and feelings make themselves known to me. Suddenly, (sometimes even days later) when I least expect it, into my head pops a new idea or a solution I had been seeking. Other times something wonderful happens. Some might think it's just plain luck but I *know* it's because I had already created it in my mind.

Is daydreaming a pointless distraction? I think not. Everything starts as someone's daydream.

What are your wildest dreams? Don't be afraid to blue sky; be open to anything that could bring more joy into your life.

Nothing makes you want something more than being able to visualize yourself having it. The more you visualize what you want the more likely you will put in place what you need in order to get it. Whether it's a vacation exploring ancient cities in Europe, a new deck on your house, a health goal or anything else that stirs you — get out the scissors and glue and get creative. It's arts and crafts time.

Put your dreams on a Vision Board. While some might think of it as a bit *woo-woo*, it works. The garden I tend, the vacations I take and the memories I make were all once on my board.

Believe the vision of what your life will become and see your future unfold as you intend.

wear your life well

knock on the door

When one door of happiness closes, another opens; but often we look so long at the closed door that we don't see the one that has opened for us.

~ Helen Keller

When the doors of the store closed for the last time I walked away from working the floors in fashion retail — forever.

As fate would have it, one of the lifestyle reporters for the *Calgary Herald* called to tell me that the Publisher asked her if she knew anyone who could plan a wedding for a friend. "I gave him your name," she said. "You will be getting a call." I informed her that I had never done this type of thing before but I would be interested in giving it a try. It sounded like fun.

The meeting time wasn't opportune for me; I had to shuffle some other things around to make it work. I had no idea what to expect and was quite naïve about the world of professional event planners.

When I was buzzed into the parkade I was given the code to the personal elevator which would take me directly into the bride and groom's sprawling, two-storey penthouse in the heart of Calgary, near Prince's Island Park.

WOW. I was glad they couldn't see my 10-year-old Chrysler K-car (with a dent). I couldn't help but wonder *just who these people were?*

I knocked. When the door opened I was greeted by a middle-aged man, small in stature, with a big smile and an abundance of presence. He welcomed me into his home and introduced himself and his fiancée.

That first meeting lasted well over an hour. I knew it was an interview, but it never felt that way. The tone was relaxed — and they were gracious. Together we began to explore the possibilities of what could be.

They never asked me about my event management experience — I felt obliged to tell them I had never done *anything* like this before. Their response was "We believe you can. We like your ideas and want you to be the person to plan the celebration of our marriage."

I was hired to create a one-of-a-kind experience for a three-day event. It was to be held at the grandiose castle in the Rockies: the world-renowned Fairmont Banff Springs Hotel.

Over the years I had seen this hotel, that rises like a magical, medieval structure in the soaring mountains, many times. I had never been inside and never, ever imagined I would be coming back to stay; nor that it would become a pillar in my life.

The three of us met every Monday evening at 7:00 for the next year to plan this extravaganza. I was assured that the only limitation might be my imagination. There was no budget. They wanted me to create the ultimate, world-class experience for their guests and a wonderful, warm memory for them. I was now playing in the leagues of "the lifestyles of the rich and famous."

So, who were these people? It wasn't until our second meeting that I discovered that he was President and CEO of an international chemicals corporation. With an oil-based economy, Calgary is head office to many major companies. Before long, he

58

made it known to his colleagues — all prominent Calgary business leaders — that I was *the* person they needed to engage to execute events of significant social importance for both personal and corporate celebrations.

I was busy with my moonlighting careers: writing, speaking, teaching and now event management. I knew it was time to give up my day job. I could no longer dedicate a full day at work and manage the other responsibilities as well. I was reasonably sure I could pay my bills and so said good-bye to the security of a regular paycheck.

Opportunity knocks — sometimes it's not the right time, other times you might not feel as though you have the experience — but always, always, always answer the door. You just never know what opportunity awaits you on the other side.

wear your life well

do it for you

You said you 'n' me was gonna get out of town and for once just really let our hair down. Well darlin' look out cause my hair is comin' down.

~Thelma Dickerson, *Thelma & Louise*

The idea of a weekend away with some girlfriends appealed to me.

I did some research to find out what might be available and discovered the trend was for boot-camp-getaways where you eat lettuce all weekend and work out for hours.

No wine.

No fun.

No appeal.

After all, I don't have that kind of strict discipline at home so why would I want to pay a lot of money to go away and feel deprived and inadequate? Surely, I wasn't the only woman looking for a different kind of experience.

With my background in Program Design and Event Planning I had the perfect skill set to create an event. I made a list of what was important to me:

- Don't have to count calories or glasses of wine
- Luxurious hotel and surroundings
- Meet new like-minded women and spend time with old friends

- An environment where multi-generations of women would feel comfortable

- Seminars for renewal and fun

- Not an "I'm going to achieve weekend"

- Me time. A chance to chill out

- Don't want to feel like I have to be better — just be me

- Want to let my hair down and have fun

- Find a way to make a difference in the lives of women

And out of this list I created the *Ultimate Pajama Party* ®. I broached the idea with my editor at the *Calgary Herald* in the hopes that I could get the newspaper to be my sponsor. The answer was a resounding YES.

In the years that followed the story of the pajama party became a media darling with items featured not only in local publications but nationally as well — papers such as *The Globe and Mail*, *National Post* and even in U.S. media: The *Wall Street Journal*, *Cincinnati Enquirer*, WNBC *Today* in New York and *MORE Magazine*.

In 1996 I took the concept of a pajama party out of the rec room to create an event for grown-up girls at the rustic yet luxurious Fairmont Jasper Park Lodge. I didn't create that first event with the idea of making money, it was a passion project, but soon it became a business — the business of making women happy.

With my daughter Lisa by my side, we wore our hearts to work and the event grew exponentially — hosting annual events over the next 15 years at a number of Fairmont resort and city properties across Canada and even tropical locations such as Bermuda. The *Caribbean Princess* was the ship where women would *escape completely*® with us as we set sail for week-long adventures together.

At each event hundreds of women were re-experiencing the pajama party pleasures of their youth — blissful times away from home, hanging out with friends, eating, talking, laughing and staying up half the night. The event drew everyone from mothers and adult daughters, sisters, groups from work, to "five best friends from junior high" who hadn't reconnected in many years. Women came alone, in pairs, and in groups, to shake the rattle of everyday life knowing that they wouldn't have to make the beds, do the dishes, put out the trash or do one last load of laundry in the daily drudge.

With success came setbacks. Managing all the aspects at a distance presented its own set of challenges from money to manpower. When Fairmont Jasper Park Lodge approached me with an offer to purchase the event I knew it would be the right thing for its continued long-term survival. Fairmont has taken it to another level with celebrities like Canadian Singer/Songwriters Jann Arden and Chantal Kreviazuk and American Actress Molly Ringwald (star of *Sixteen Candles* and *Pretty in Pink*) hosting the hundreds of women who attend each year. The legacy lives on.

I never dreamed my concept would have such a wide reach and be such a transformative event for so many women. By building what is important to me, I clarified my own values and goals. As a result, my own journey has been life-changing for them.

My definition of success is to do work that you love, with people you love, for people you love. But more important is the mark I leave behind. I am humbled and happy knowing that thousands of women have participated, and will continue to celebrate each other — for each other's sake.

Be you. Do your thing. Whatever you do, make sure it makes you happy.

say YES to being a rock star

Some guy said to me: "Don't you think you're too old to sing rock n' roll?"
I said: "You'd better check with Mick Jagger."

~Cher

Beatles or Stones?

During elementary school I collected Beatle cards — the kind that came in five-cent, bubble-gum packages. I really wasn't interested in *all* of the Beatles, just Paul McCartney, so I would trade several other Beatle cards for one Paul card. I thought Paul was cute.

Decades later as Stones guitarist Ron Wood was walking toward me with his signature old-rocker swagger I wasn't thinking he was cute — but I was star struck. After all some say that the Rolling Stones have become the most important band in rock and roll history.

I was hosting the Saturday Night Gala Dinner for the *Ultimate Pajama Party ®,* which was being held at the Fairmont Chateau Lake Louise in the Canadian Rockies, when the hotel special events manager motioned me out of the room. It wasn't a run-of-the-mill pop-by to see if everything was fine and to find out if anything else was needed. It was the moment that I met Ron Wood along with his back-up singer Bernard Fowler and two burly body guards. I learned that they were staying at the posh resort for a few days of down-time before the next leg of the 2005 Rolling Stones World Tour promoting their new album, *A Bigger Bang.* Mick Jagger and Keith Richards were elsewhere.

Ron had been wandering the hotel and was drawn by loud music and lots of laughter. He wondered if it would be okay to have a table brought to the back of the room so the four of them could just hang out and enjoy the fun.

I said YES.

There were almost 200 gals at that event: no guys — except my son Chris who was our official event photographer. We had live, local entertainment but our budget wasn't flush enough for a back-up band so the music Ron had heard was all Karaoke.

His security staff made sure that I understood the ground rules. No rushing and no photographs. I went back into the ballroom and made the announcement. The women were already partying like rock stars — drinking and dancing — when Ron and his entourage slipped quietly into the back of the room.

Soon (feeling safe in his surroundings) he got up and started to mix and mingle. After he partied with our group for about three hours he wanted to bid us a good night with a turn at the Karaoke microphone.

I explained that I had a professional photographer in the room and asked if he could take a couple of photos. Agreed.

I was making the announcement about what was about to happen when Ron took the microphone from my hand, kissed me on the cheek and performed his rendition of The Temptations' *My Girl*.

Chris had been taking group shots of girlfriends throughout the evening. He got ready to shoot Ron and Bernard performing; one shot and his camera battery died. One was all it took.

Our media partner *Lite 96* had their morning DJ in attendance. The news of Ron's surprise appearance was all over the air waves early Monday. Newspapers got wind of the fact that he had crashed the pajama party and they contacted me for an interview and photo. The story with the headline "Lone Stone rolls in the Rockies" (*Calgary Herald*, Tuesday, October 25, 2005) ran in newspapers across the country that week and made its way into the next edition of *STAR* magazine — the American tabloid that prides itself in breaking celebrity news first.

Rock stars show up and shine. Rock stars share their gift with people. It was immaterial that Ron Wood was a guitarist in a famous band and that he rakes in mega-bucks from concerts while touring. That evening he showed us he is like everyone else. He beamed with happiness while he enjoyed the moments and shared his music with us.

You don't have to be famous to be a rock star. The idea that being super-rich and famous will make you happy is hype. There are rock stars in each of us. Whether we are ever on a magazine cover or in the headlines isn't significant.

Become a star in your own eyes. Give it your all, work hard and find ways to follow your passions. Live your dreams and the money will follow.

That's my rock star aspiration.

wear your life well

reinvent yourself

One day Alice came to a fork in the road and saw a Cheshire cat in a tree.

"Which road do I take?" she asked.
"Where do you want to go?" was his response.
"I don't know," Alice answered.
"Then," said the cat, "it doesn't matter."

~Lewis Carroll's *Alice's Adventures in Wonderland*

I've always been a curious person mostly led by my heart. I'll probably never stop asking myself what I want to be when I grow up. Even so, I know myself well enough to understand that I am highly creative and get bored easily. That is why I've always had at least three side-gigs on the go at any given time. I'm interested in a lot of things and am always open to new experiences.

Even though I've had a life-long career in fashion, sometimes circumstances would merge calling me to redirect my fate completely. An unexpected turn of events has often sparked my reinvention.

Now working outside the retail world — a world where so many work so hard and without the training, support and appreciation they deserve — I determined that I would make a contribution by creating a training program for Retail Fashion Consultants. I had already piloted the concept with five-star evaluations as an 80-hour certificate program at the Southern Alberta Institute of Technology (now SAIT Polytechnic). It was time to take it out into the real world.

Retail has never been an easy business. My program, *InCredible Selling,* is much more than just another sales and customer service program. It's a system that combines the fundamentals of fashion and image consulting with successful selling strategies. The result: Retail Fashion Consultants who have the skill and confidence to turn a one-time buyer into a lifetime client.

Getting fashion retailers to invest was more difficult than I had imagined. The response to the need and specifics of the skills I would teach was overwhelmingly positive. But, I soon ascertained that retail stores were short-sighted when it came to staff development. I was single-minded in my determination but I was fighting to change a culture that didn't understand the long-term payoff of investing in its people. I taught at a few independent boutiques but had yet to land a major department store and, honestly, I was starting to give up.

At that time Eaton's — a 130-year-old Canadian chain — was struggling with what was more than just a long-term slump in sales. The store needed a makeover and put 10's of millions of dollars into branding in order to re-launch itself as a more upscale, hip fashion center. I knew first-hand that it's not advertising that creates a satisfied customer — it's the actual experience. Opening new fashion departments, creating glossy magazine advertising, and producing a barrage of television commercials were words and images, but their promise had to deliver.

I thought their new strategy was smart — I still do. My expertise was a perfect fit. I was able to reinforce for them that *any* store can assemble a sales staff to go out on the floor but if Eaton's staff was seen as outstanding the store would prosper. I started a training program in Calgary and soon a buzz started about the work I was doing. Even outside the industry the word was spreading. I was awarded the prestigious Global Television/YWCA *Woman of Vision* award in the category of Business and Entrepreneurship and a television segment was produced about my pioneering work.

Getting ready to move into the Edmonton market, which meant a provincial presence, I still had my sights set on getting a meeting with head office in Toronto. I imagined that if it went well I might have a shot at a national contract — and the opportunity to be an integral part of the bigger picture and of their ultimate success. But I started to worry when I saw a lot of clearance merchandize in their aisles. The Toronto meeting never happened. Operational and financial issues hindered the turnaround. Eaton's landed in bankruptcy court. Ultimately there wasn't enough time for the repositioning plan to work.

Eaton's closing kicked my butt. Yes, it did.

I stood on the sidelines of my life having a "chic happens" moment while standing at the intersection of change and chance.

I was in my 40s when life as I knew it shifted and something inside of me did as well. Ready or not the next reinvention was about to happen. The opportunity to re-design my life (again) terrified me. My outer life and inner life were mirrors of each other. No longer was I simply an older version of my younger self, I was about to become a different woman; a woman in a new stage of life. I didn't want to recover and return to normal. I wanted to bounce forward and find a new path.

For many years, my sense of self was stitched to my work. I was having an identity crisis. Without the mantle of my *fashion* persona, (which over the years had become an extension of me) I was forced to add a new dimension of self-discovery: Who am I, *really*?

For a while I was in mourning. Grief isn't only about death. It's relevant to anything you become attached to or separated from. I found it hard to step away from something I loved and to say good-bye to the person I used to be.

I told myself over and over again "Relax, it's going to be okay. It really is. Just relax." It was time to breathe, to trust, to make the next move, to let go and see what happens.

I accepted what happened as a cue pointing me in a new direction. I discovered that my life is bigger than any one experience and the sum of all my experiences is my life. During this time of mayhem Scottie and I were also in the midst of renovating our newly-purchased home. I confessed (in the hot tub after several glasses of wine) that lately I was having a lot more fun in Home Depot than I was at Holt Renfrew. I decided to make a big, bold, paradigm shift to evolve my career trajectory to include selling real estate.

A kick in the butt was a good thing for me. It moved me to release the old and outdated view of myself and take a closer look at the strands that stitch my destiny together in a more expansive way.

And I'm not done yet.

When was the last time you reinvented yourself?

And when will be the next time?

find joy on the journey

May your choices reflect your hopes, not your fears.

~Nelson Mandela

No matter what choices we make, our destiny has more to do with how we see things than the circumstances in which we find ourselves. Happiness is a choice. Let yourself be happy.

Seriously.

Who can know what the right decision is? There are many roads and many detours. Most often we find the right path. But sometimes there are missteps. We may never understand the who, what and *wear* (I couldn't resist) of life but when we accept that we will never find all the answers, we CAN change how we see happiness.

Some decisions are comfortable and effortless. Others may require compromise and choice and cause us to think intently and at length. Ultimately, no matter how courageous it might be to make a choice, the only thing that matters is that we do — and that means sticking with our decisions about what is right for us.

Aristotle said, "There is only one way to avoid criticism: do nothing, say nothing, and be nothing." Sad but true. Some people will look down on us for our life decisions, no matter what they are. But remember. When our sense of satisfaction is derived from the opinions of others we are letting them tell us who we are. Don't give that power to any person. Never forget who you are.

Do you think it's hard to do? I put forth that it's simple — but not easy. Think about the life you want and live a life true to you, not a life others expect of you. Authenticity leads to happiness and being happy never goes out of style. Actress, style icon and humanitarian Audrey Hepburn advocated that "the most important thing is to enjoy your life — to be happy — it's all that matters."

lessons from the journey

get into change shape

express your essence

find your groove

decide your destiny

start where you are

believe that good things are on their way

forget about being perfect

mind your thoughts

believe in day dreams

knock on the door

do it for you

say YES to being a rock star

reinvent yourself

find joy on the journey

Download bonus *wear your life well* content at

www.wearyourlifewell.com

wear your life well

fashion
your style

wear your life well

make room for a new you

I like my money right where I can see it ... hanging in my closet.

~Carrie (Sex and the City)

How long has it been since you cleaned out your closet?

What is it that keeps us from clearing the clutter in our lives?

It is an exercise that is about much more than culling the clothes that no longer fit our bodies. Ultimately we are asking ourselves whether our clothes still fit our life or if we are ready to make a necessary life change. Over time our tastes change as we grow and evolve and it's good to let go of the things that no longer serve us. When we clarify our needs and simplify our space we realize that sometimes we are just hanging onto things that no longer inspire joy.

The juxtaposition of nothing to wear and no room in your burst-at-the-seams closet is most definitely a girl thing. When digging through your clothes starts to feel like you are looking for the doorway to Narnia, it's time to get ruthless and decide to discard. If you are like many women, you probably have items still bearing the price tag and shoes you have never worn.

Opening your closet door and rooting through it for *something* you know is in there — somewhere — takes the fun out of getting dressed. Keep your closets organized and go through the process of editing at least once a year. It's almost impossible to put together a cohesive outfit if you can't even see what is in there.

The challenge is deciding what stays and what goes. Start by sorting through your clothes and putting them into one of three piles:

What You Wear

All the things you are wearing currently and enjoying can go into this pile. Most women wear a small number of outfits most of the time. This pile should be the *no-brainer* garments that you feel comfortable wearing whenever you put them on. Do take note if you have a tendency to buy too much of the same thing. How many pairs of black pants do you need? Is it important to have four pink sweaters? You don't need to get rid of these things, but be aware of what you already have next time you shop and find yourself looking for more of the same.

What Needs Repair

Take clothes that you never got around to altering to a tailor or seamstress. It might be a black dress that needs to be lengthened, pants that need to be shortened or a zipper that needs to be replaced. Don't bother if it's a garment that has to be completely rebuilt in order to fit you. That's too expensive and it likely won't work anyway.

Time to Toss

Some items are an easy decision. They include that great deal you couldn't pass up. It was on triple-mark-down and shouldn't have been bought in the first place.

Some things are harder to part with. Wine helps. If you are not wearing them, take them out of your closet. Out of sight, out of mind. Put them in a box or in another closet. If you don't have to reinstate them in the next six months, it's a pretty safe bet that you won't miss them.

It's hard to admit to ourselves that some garments no longer fit and probably never will again. I commiserate. I know first-hand that your sagging self-esteem will be elevated each and every morning when you are NOT looking at them as a reminder.

Also include all the clothes that don't match anything else. If you love them enough, make one or two trips to see if you can find something. Since this type of clothing is rarely a basic, the likelihood is limited. Most colors after a year or more become obscure, they are a slightly different shade and you'll never really find a great match. If you do, lucky you!

Don't even think of keeping items that are outdated hoping that they will be back in style someday. If you wore a garment the first time around and drag it out of the closet again people will think you haven't bought any new clothes in the last 25 years. If you find a look you love that reminds you of something you once wore, purchase the new version. The looks may be similar, but the fabrics and interpretations are fresh — the difference is quite subtle but definitely noticeable.

I have conducted many closet interventions when asked.   I understand that it is important to let go of things that no longer serve a purpose. When we detox our closet clutter it's like a detox for the mind. If we ponder why we have a hard time letting go we come to understand that it's either about an attachment to the past or a fear for the future. Living in the here and now — this moment in time — gives us a calm mindset that allows us to create the life (and wardrobe) we want.

Space is one of the most luxurious things you can have in your closet and your head. Putting your closet in order will lighten your load in life.

wear your life well

recognize your value

Someone out there is looking for exactly what you've got and will never try and undercut your value or question your worth. Some things in life just can't be bartered over or placed on the sale rack — and your self worth is at the top of the list.

~Mandy Hale

Most women don't see fashion as life-changing. Many are not interested in the whole *fashion thing* at all. For years I didn't understand that working with women *playing dress-up* matters.

I would assure my clients that if they didn't identify with the looks on the runway that season it was just fine. Neither did I.

There are two distinct views when it comes to the importance of fashion in our lives. Oscar Wilde opines fashion "is a form of ugliness so intolerable that we have to alter it every *six* months." Personally, I agree with Designer Christian Lacroix who tells us that "Fashion is like a television screen on the world."

Obviously there needs to be a balance between the two schools of thought.

Fashion is art. Style is story.

Runway looks and fashion photography are intended to knock us off-balance so that we will be ready to accept something new in a more modified version. Designers don't really expect us to wear clothing the way they show it; instead we are expected to use it as inspiration. The challenge is to open our minds to consider something new.

In the store, I offered my expertise and would translate my philosophy of getting dressed to help a woman differentiate perception from reality. It was a light-hearted experience and I illuminated how easy it was for her to look great as I deciphered various fashion conundrums. I witnessed profound personal transformations, inside and out, as a more confident self-image and a more stylish woman emerged.

I got heartfelt thanks, notes of appreciation and sometimes even flowers from my clients — external validation. In the early days of my career I was astonished that even the well-heeled women saw my value, not just as a woman who worked in fashion retail but as someone they looked to for guidance and advice often on matters beyond clothes. In an *aha* moment I realized that my self-worth had nothing to do with my craft. I couldn't do what they did — and they couldn't do what I did. We all have different gifts. So, I took myself off the discount rack.

I began to understand how much I had to give through my expertise and also through my energy and spirit. I gave of myself abundantly and it was returned to me generously.

Others appreciate the contributions you make, even if you can't see them yourself. My biggest breakthrough moment was the realization that my calling was to help generations of women make friends with themselves through fashion.

Even if you don't think what you do matters — it does. It's not what you do — it's why you do it that is meaningful.

Do it with passion and care.

claim your confidence

beautiful *(byoo-ta -fal) adjective*
1 combination of all the qualities of a person that delight the senses and mind. 2 lovely, charming, delightful, pleasing. 3 attractive woman 4. you

How do we define beauty? Is it from the inside out or the outside in? They go together like fine food and good wine in a perfect pairing.

As women, why is it so easy to doubt ourselves? Perhaps the media images of flawless beauties and exaggerated stories of women who have and do it all play a part in our collective neurosis. Deep down we know that those images are air brushed and no one can have it all and be everything to everyone. It's impossible. Yet, we expect perfection from ourselves. Ultimately what matters is not about how the world judges us but rather how we judge ourselves.

Have you ever noticed if you are not feeling confident and you doubt even one teeny tiny thing about yourself, suddenly everything is magnified exponentially? You start out thinking that there is something wrong with your hair, your body, your clothes and pretty soon it's about your relationship, your work, your abilities, your health, and *gasp* pretty much everything in your life.

I am finally okay with the fact that I am no better, no worse, than anyone else and that I am a work in progress. I'm more comfortable with who I am now than I was when I was younger. I know that if I focus my energy toward reaching my potential, and cherish myself in the process, I will claim my beauty and feel my power. I am doing the best I can at this moment in my life, given my circumstances, and what I now know.

I am learning to appreciate myself for who I am and who I will become.

Being a stylish woman isn't about looking chic or being superficial. It's about discovering yourself, owning your look and showing up for yourself in life.

Where do you start and how do you find it? Your closet contains so much more than your clothes. Clothing is an extension of who you are, what you are thinking and how you are feeling. Getting dressed is as much for the spirit and psyche as it is for the body. When you pay attention to the outside, it also sparks something on the inside.

Spirit and style are attributes you already have. You don't have to change who you are. Quite the opposite. You just need to fully embrace the woman you are.

Diane Von Furstenberg reminds us: Character. Intelligence. Strength. Style. THAT MAKES BEAUTY.

stay true to yourself

Style is a way to say who you are without having to speak.

~Rachel Zoe

Do your clothes tell the story of who you are? The right clothes can simultaneously cover you and bare you. Once you can hold on to the core of who you are, change can be a welcome adventure. Dressing like yourself will help you to be more yourself.

When you go shopping it doesn't matter what your friend or the sales associate says. They might love the look and think it's great but often they are looking at it through their self-filter. While you value their opinion ultimately what you think and feel is what is important. When you stand in front of the mirror ask yourself "Does this look like *me*?" If it does you'll wear it often. If not, it will gather dust in the back of the closet because you will find it emotionally exhausting to wear.

This exercise will give you a glimpse into the true you. Sometimes several looks might seem to fit you, depending upon your mood. This is because we are a composite of fashion personalities in varying degrees.

Think of the look that is most like you most of the time. This is your primary fashion personality or your comfort zone. Don't think of the answers in terms of should; choose answers that sing to your soul.

Your personality evolves. Evaluate your preferences throughout your life and you'll understand your unique style story.

Here are some questions to think about. Write down an answer that is based not on what you *should* wear but rather something that makes you feel good.

- If you were going to a gala dinner and black tie affair and your body could wear it, what would you wear?

- Assuming your hair would actually co-operate and it was flattering to your face shape, what hair style would you choose?

- What kind of make-up makes you most comfortable?

- Assuming you have a perfect body and you could wear anything, how would you like your clothing to fit?

- How would you describe your walk and gestures?

- Describe your physical size, stature and stance.

- You just won a shopping spree to indulge in your fantasy piece of clothing. What would you buy?

- Describe your jewelry.

- What would be the best compliment you would hear from your friends?

Which of these fashion personalities best describes you?

CLASSIC

This woman doesn't want to be labelled or stand out. She embodies chic perfectly. Her mannerisms are nearly as discreet as her clothing. Her style is understated and "simply the best" is what she wears. She does not like gimmicks and makes a conscious effort to invest in clothing that lasts.

BUZZ WORDS: Structured, understated, chic, refined, polished. HAIRSTYLE: Simple, neat, soft, medium length, controlled. FASHION DESIGN: Trim, elegant, dignified. FABRIC: Plain textures, solid colors. She rarely wears prints and loves a monochromatic look. ACCESSORIES: Simple, modest, always genuine, inconspicuous. FASHION CHALLENGE: Don't always be so safe and conservative. Use some fashion savvy; otherwise you risk looking boring and uninspired.

NATURAL
This woman is casual and relaxed and believes that comfort is foremost. She is approachable and draws people to her easily. She prefers pants over skirts and separates over suits. She doesn't like to be noticed and uses restraint in design.

BUZZ WORDS: Casual, relaxed, unstructured, unpretentious, informal. HAIRSTYLE: Windblown, easy-care, casual, nothing fussy. FASHION DESIGN: Sportswear-inspired, jeans, separates, simple lines, always comfortable. FABRIC: Wash and wear, interesting textures, plaid and prints. ACCESSORIES: Simple and small, metal and minimal. FASHION CHALLENGE: Take care pulling your look together. You want to look natural not necessarily *be* natural. Don't forget to put some effort into pulling yourself together.

ROMANTIC
This woman has a soft elegance and beauty. She appreciates sentimental value. She prefers fluid fabrics and draped garments or lightly tailored garments with silky blouses and soft sweaters. Her jewellery is dainty in detail but lavish in effect. She loves pretty things, colors and must avoid the tendency to overdress. BUZZ WORDS: Beautiful, soft, sensuous, charming, pretty, feminine. HAIRSTYLE: Soft waves, feathered cuts, full, usually medium to long length. Often wears pretty hair accessories.

FASHION DESIGN: Flowing, lightly tailored, feminine. FABRIC: Softly draping, detailed, lace, floral prints, soft colors. ACCESSORIES: Dainty, sparkly, lavish and ornate. FASHION CHALLENGE: Don't overdo your look. Too much of a good thing isn't better. Be careful not to look too girly-girl especially as you mature.

DRAMATIC

This woman is accepting of change and is always ahead of the game. Her signature is simple, plain clothing that makes a statement through color, geometric pattern or strong contrasts. She loves original, large, look-at-me accessories. She stands out in a crowd – and wants to.

BUZZ WORDS: Outrageous, unique, trendy, dazzling, eye-catching. HAIRSTYLE: Severe, avant garde, any length, strong or interesting color. Interesting angles. FASHION DESIGN: Bold, tailored and exotic, slinky and exotic. FABRICS: Silky, shiny, matt and mannish. Sheer and sumptuous or heavy. Whatever makes a statement very a-la-mood. ACCESSORIES: Simple, large, heavy and unique. FASHION CHALLENGE: Don't over-do your look. You don't want to intimidate others or stand out so much that you don't fit in.

There are no right or wrong combinations and any combination is possible. That's what makes you unique. Your fashion personality evolves over the years, just as you do. You might find that you are a bit of each personality, or one dominant personality, or two equal personalities. So you might be primarily a Classic personality with a touch of Romantic or have similarities in several categories meaning you are quite comfortable in all those looks.

This is a fun concept to work with if you are looking to do a bit of a makeover. For example, if your primary personality is NATURAL and the second most-like-you personality is DRAMATIC you can feel safe that adding touches of dramatic to your wardrobe won't threaten your comfort zone.

On the other hand, if you are a strong NATURAL and have no ROMANTIC in you at all, don't go down that road for a new look. You won't feel comfortable or like what you see in the mirror.

What's your combination? Oprah is a Dramatic/Romantic. Michelle Obama is Classic/Natural. Ellen DeGeneres is Natural/Natural. Angelina Jolie is Classic/ Romantic.

You can learn even more about your distinct style persona by keeping a visual portfolio in a progress journal. Even if you are not a regular fashion magazine buyer, pick up a few of the latest. Flip through the pages in the comfort of your home. There doesn't need to be an ounce of reality involved because you can "pretend buy" anything on the page. It doesn't matter what's in your wallet; it's all about inspiration.

Go ahead, find the looks you love and tear out those pages. Paste them in a scrapbook, put them in a file or just lay them out on a table to see the pattern in the puzzle that is you. The results are often a real revelation. What are the visuals telling you? Ask yourself: Are these outfits similar to what you are wearing now, or are you yearning for a new look? Do these outfits have more color or less color that you normally wear? Are you more attracted to certain silhouettes and styles? Are you favouring prints over plain? Is it the way outfits are accessorized that you find interesting? What is consistent in these looks? What is the common denominator?

As you flip through the pages you'll start to see your fashion spirit. It's a great way to navigate trends and stay aware of your own style evolution. Fashion says "me too" but style says "only me."

Diana Vreeland reminds us that *it's not the dress you wear, but the life you live in that dress* that matters.

learn to say NO

The shoe that fits one person pinches another; there is no recipe for living that suits all cases.

Each of us carries our own life-plan, which cannot be superseded by any other.

~C.G. Jung

Nothing makes me crankier than a pair of shoes that hurt. I can't believe that I spent so many years working in the fashion world shod in shoes that put me in severe pain at the end of the day. Presenting an elegant exterior is not without its perils. I look around today and see many fashion-forward women teetering on their stilettos and am reminded of the discomfort that intolerable footwear affords.

Men just don't seem to get why we love the many facets of shoes so much. Each pair is like a friend with a distinct personality. Some make us feel glamorous and sexy, others chic and sophisticated and still others casual and funky. We *need* shoes that have both style and function — the basics — boots, an evening shoe, classic pumps, ballet flats, casual shoes, sandals and sneakers. Then there are the shoes we *want*. How many pair we own is limited by our budget and closet space. Some only hold a place in our imaginations. A woman — and her shoes — is a beautiful thing.

Shoes always make me feel good. Whether I am fitting into my skinny pants or my fat pants, my foot size stays the same. Shoes never make me feel fat. But, I wish there could be more shoes that are cute, sexy, stylish *and* comfortable.

When I have to decide between cute and comfortable, most often I go with comfortable. I understand *me* and know that happy feet equal a happy face. I am grateful that one of the good things about getting older is finding the courage to just say NO. Now, I've traded those silly stilettos for fabulous flats.

Living authentically is about having what means most to you — on *your* terms. Although it can feel uncomfortable to say NO, if we do things because we think we should in order to please others we sacrifice our comfort — and may even cripple our life.

Saying NO is one of the most transformative life skills that you can master. It allows you to step ahead of the things and people that don't support or inspire you.

In *The Wizard of Oz* Dorothy established that a new pair of shoes can change lives magically. And Glinda, The Good Witch, reminds us that "you had the power all along, my dear."

Create your life. Take one step at a time and follow the yellow-brick road to the place of your dreams.

(Since it's a brick road you might want to wear light-weight hikers instead of ruby high heels.)

reveal your true colors

Nature always wears the colors of the spirit.

~Ralph Waldo Emerson

"Purple, Grandma. Purple." Even at a young age, my granddaughter Zoë had a definite opinion of what she wanted to wear on those occasions when I helped her to get dressed. For her, it was all about the color purple. I know that purple makes her happy. She told me so.

Because of my background in fashion, I have worked closely with women to help them identify their perfect color palette based on the natural colorings of their hair, skin and eyes. I don't believe we need to get stuck in rules, but I do believe it's good to know which color choices make us look more radiant.

Yet, even if a color might be good for us, why is it that we feel comfortable with some colors and not with others? Color psychology is the key. It's natural to gravitate to particular colors that are a reflection of our innermost thoughts and feelings. While our preferences may change throughout the years the colors we favour are always an accurate indicator of what is going on in our psyche.

Our color preferences reveal a lot about our personalities and from the dawn of culture to the present day people have developed strong associations with specific hues. The colors around us influence us at a subconscious level whether we realize it or not. While there is no universally accepted theory, color psychologists agree that colors affect our mood and influence our emotions.

Me. I love blue. Any shade of blue — but especially that mysterious, rich, deep tone of a dusky midnight blue. I don't know why I like blue so much but I do know that when I wear it I feel safe and self-confident. When I wear blue I am happy. Maybe it's because that when I was a small girl my mother dressed me mostly in blue. She would give me a hug and tell me she liked me in blue because it made my eyes look even bluer than they are. She still tells me that today.

Each color evokes an emotional response from us and it's not the same for everyone. Every color has positive and negative attributes. For example, blue can represent calm, trust, honesty and security. It can also be perceived as stuffy, boring, lacking in spontaneity, old.

Years ago, I came home with a new suit that was a magnificent shade of robin's egg blue. As soon as I saw it I fell in love with it and knew I had to have it. It was a fantastic color, fit and fabric. When I got home I was excited to model it for Scottie. He complimented the fit but was less than enthusiastic overall. Why? You can imagine my dismay when he shared with me that *that* particular shade of blue reminded him of the clothing his grandmother used to wear. Not something I wanted to hear from a man who is six years my junior! I decided to return the suit and keep the man. Blue is still my comfort color, my favorite color. I just don't wear *that particular shade* of old-lady blue anymore.

As for my little purple princess Zoë, I know she will love purple until that day in the future, 50 years or so from now, when someone calls it menopause mauve.

live a colorful life

*I'll see your true colors and that's why I love you, so don't be
afraid to let them show
Your true colors, true colors are beautiful, like a rainbow*

~Cyndi Lauper

I admit that I'm a recovering black-o-holic. We all seem to have a
love affair with black. Maybe it's an addiction or maybe we've just
been hanging on to that security blanket for too many years. It's
just so easy so get out of bed in the morning and reach for black.

We all know that black is more forgiving of figure realities, goes
with everything, works for almost any occasion and satisfies
almost any style and mood. We can wear it year-round no matter
what the weather or the event. Black can convey many states of
mind: modest, sophisticated or sultry. Even grief. And a red wine
spill won't ruin a little black dress.

With all black's attributes, I still caution you to wear colorful
clothing. Yes, black is the foundation of many wardrobes. But a
strength overdone is a weakness.

I appreciate that all black garments do not look alike, but unless
you are a Sicilian widow you do not need half a dozen black
jackets, a dozen pairs of black pants, two dozen pairs of black
shoes and a stack of black sweaters.

Admittedly lots of women appear to be afraid of color. But unless
we can enliven our otherwise monochromatic wardrobe with
some interesting textures, accessories and colors, we will start to
look drab and dreary. There are no absolute rules about color but

97

understanding which color choices are most flattering to you becomes more important than ever once your own coloring starts to age.

Everyone can wear every color. It is the undertone and intensity that is important. Your personal coloring is genetically determined before your birth and the basic undertone of your skin will not change, except to fade or deepen with a tan — which changes only the value of intensity, not the color. Mother nature co-ordinated your skin, eyes and hair to harmonize with each other. She didn't make any mistakes. Whatever your ethnic background, your skin has either a warm or cool base. The kindest colors for a Northern-European blonde may in fact be the best colors for an African woman.

There are qualified color consultants who have the expertise to help you discover which hues harmonize best with your personal coloring.

You can do your own version of a color test to determine whether warm or cool colors look best on you. This analysis is based on comparison and you don't need to be overly technical. You may look pretty good in some of the colors from one undertone but a lot better in the colors of another.

The Munsell Color Theory is a charting system which offers a logical and precise formula for understanding the art and science of color. This color concept is accepted universally and is used by fashion experts, paint manufacturers, interior designers — anyone who works with color.

Your selection of flattering colors is almost limitless as long as you remember to keep the undertone (blue or yellow) as the one that best suits you. The undertone of a color is defined by its base — yellow (warm) or blue (cool). When differentiating them in your mind think of red and yellow-red as being related to the warmth of the sun. Blue and purple can be found in the shadows on snow and ice and appear cool.

For example: With the color green, different undertones will create either a blue-green or a yellow-green. When you add blue, you create cool colors; adding yellow gives us warm colors.

Color clarity it also a consideration. Do you look better in a bright clear candy pink or is a subdued dusty rose more complimentary?

A word of caution: Never judge by one color alone. Always compare colors of equal intensity, but opposite undertone. For example, don't compare a pale shade to a strong intense version of the same color. Sometimes the differences are small. Decide by the best group.

Which colors look best on you?

COOL	WARM
Navy	Chocolate Brown
Grey	Camel
Forest Green	Olive Green
Burgundy	Rust
Fuchsia Pink	Orange
Silver	Gold
Pure White	Buttery Cream

Be objective. Don't be influenced by your emotional response to color. Look at your face not at the color. The right color enhances your face. Facial lines are less obvious, the skin looks glowing and your eyes sparkle. Even the whites of your eyes look whiter. The wrong colors can make you look more tired and drain the natural color from your face. Dark circles, lines and blemishes stand out more.

Once you discover which colors best compliment your skin tone, eyes and hair color you will be happy you did. The benefits will become obvious very quickly. You will not only look better but suddenly your wardrobe starts to make more sense. Everything has better mix-and-match potential because the colors harmonize and blend.

Color really is one of the best things in life that is free. It costs just as much to buy the right color as the wrong one.

So, go a little crazy, stretch out of your comfort zone and live a more colorful life.

walk on the wild side

You were wild once. Don't let them tame you.

~Isadora Duncan

Animal prints can stump even the most stylish woman. Worn correctly you'll enjoy the attention you get because you look fabulous and feel gorgeous. On the other hand, if you don't know how to pull off the look the attention you might get is likely to be side glances, snickers and sneers. When it works — it's awesome. When it doesn't — it's awful. It's all or nothing. You need to know how to wear it and what to wear it with.

Here's how:

Wear classic: Conservative lines with minimal detailing in the garment are necessary. The print is already bold enough and doesn't translate well into a complicated garment structure. A tasteful shift-style dress, a simple sweater or a knee-length straight skirt can look extremely elegant. Wear few accessories for the same reason.

Tone it down: You might wear a solid-colored neutral cardigan, that blends with your print, over that shift-style dress or that skinny pant. Don't incorporate any item that visually competes with the primary pattern.

Wear quality: Trying to pull off the style with *looks-for-less* items can make an animal print look cheap. Spend more money and invest in quality. The look is timeless so you can buy a few staple items that will last a lifetime. If it's a sweater go for cashmere, a scarf should be silk, shoes or a handbag should be leather.

Whatever you choose to buy needs to be worn with a polished and classic attitude and style.

Don't match: Only one part of your outfit should be wild; the rest should be non-animal. Mix and match with solid, basic colors only. Blacks and browns work well for an elegant look. Dark denim and even white can often create a more casual look.

Flatter your figure: An all-over animal print looks good on a toned, fit body. Every woman can incorporate animal prints into her look successfully by choosing strategically where to focus the attention. Prints draw attention to the area they cover. If your upper body is proportionally smaller than your lower body, wear the print on top paired with a solid on the bottom. If you have narrow hips a large animal print handbag is the perfect way to find balance.

You need courage to wear animal prints. They represent boldness and adventure. Step out of the box. Experiment. Go ahead, live your wildest dreams.

(Repeat this mantra: Classy and sassy *but* never trashy.)

love what you've got

Delete the negative. Accentuate the positive!

~Donna Karan

It's time to get some new clothes. Jacket. Dress. Pants. What-have-you. You go shopping, you gather some garments and into the fitting room you go with high expectations that when you leave the store you'll be strutting your stuff.

Mirror, mirror on the wall — you are not feeling fair at all.

You realize that the garments you've tried on look better on the hanger than they do on you. Nothing seems to fit. Instant angst sets in and you are convinced that your body is uniquely weird. You had the perfect fashion body once — the one with no chest, no waist, no hips, and legs that looked like they belonged to birds. You were 10 at the time.

It's fantasy to put on a garment and assume it will work for you. If you understand your body shape, and the shape of the garment, you can find the clothes that look and feel right on you. Whether you are a size 4 or 24, fit goes beyond size. It is possible to train your eye and your mind so that you choose the clothing that is a perfect fit for the body you were blessed with.

Your basic body shape is determined by your skeletal structure. You can trim and tone, but the result will be only a more trimmed and toned version of what you are now. You can change the size of your body but not its fundamental shape.

The location of your hip bone determines where you carry your weight. A woman with a tapered hip has a tiny waist in proportion to her hips and thighs. The minute she puts on weight it seems automatically to find its way to her butt. Conversely, a woman with a high hip will have great legs and slim hips but her waist is anywhere she hangs her pantyhose.

No one body type is better than another. Everyone has figure realities (not flaws) to deal with when getting dressed. It's true, we all have our body bugaboos.

The real problem isn't with the cut of the cloth.

We are surrounded by über-images of youthful beauty in a world of unrealistic beauty standards. With age comes wisdom, or at least a reality check, and I'm learning that I'll never start feeling great about myself and learn to love all the "imperfections" that make me, ME until I stop comparing myself not only to others but to my younger self as well.

In my 20 plus years as a fashion therapist I came to know a lot about women from the other side of the dressing room door. It was not surprising to me that most women felt insecure about their bodies, but what did surprise me was that their negative body image often had little to do with what I actually saw. What they felt about their body was not what the outside world saw. No matter how large or small there was always something about their body they didn't like. Countless women declared themselves too fat or too thin. They obsessed about various body parts, their hip size, their rounded stomach, the thickness of their ankles and other assorted wobbly bits. What they were really worried about was the fact that they didn't fit into the so-called societal norm which has no basis in reality. Bottom line: they thought they would never measure up.

I am no different. I struggle with the same demons of negative self-talk and the advances of aging are complicating things even more. Why is it that when I look into a full-length mirror I zone right in on what I hate most about my body? I focus on it so intently that all I see is what I don't like. To make matters worse, I compare the worst part of myself to the best part of someone else. It could be someone who is a different size, height and weight, even someone on the cover of a magazine who has been "perfected." Then I conclude that I am not good enough. That affects me in all areas of my life.

It was easy for me to look at my clients objectively and to help them put on clothing that would enhance and express them as beautiful, interesting, complex and capable women. Why couldn't they see the same person in the mirror that I did?

So now, when I look in the mirror, I try to see myself with the same kind of acceptance that I gave my clients. I have good days and some not-so-good-days. Deep down I know that those who love me don't consider numbers on the scale or the shape of my body. The only judge who withholds love from me is ME.

I know that sometimes my insecurities hold me back so I challenge myself every time I look in the mirror to simply accept my body for what it is right now and to be happy in my own skin.

If you are ready to break from this fettering behaviour the next time you look in the mirror be gentle with yourself. Be forgiving. Let go of the need to criticize; just look at yourself and show yourself a little kindness. Become your own imaginary friend and pay yourself a compliment.

When you abandon the fear that you will never measure up, you will finally accept that you are loveable just the way you are. Self acceptance is the key to a happier life.

We come in different shapes and sizes. It's time we celebrated our various complexities in all the wondrous forms we take.

treat yourself gently

To me beauty is about being comfortable in your own skin. It's about knowing and accepting who you are.

~Ellen DeGeneres

Eventually the day comes when we no longer recognize that girl in the mirror and we would be happy to get back the figure we complained about for years.

Living a good life may mean having a few extra pounds. We're mature. We get to eat. But weight gain is the number one reason that many women give up on their style. Whether we are having a fat day (or year) the secret is to stay away from the gym clothes as daywear and give ourselves a boost by wearing things that fit well and make us feel pretty. Ignore the urge to just give up and be grateful that something — anything — fits.

Life is too short and precious to be spent in a holding pattern until we have lost the pounds. Stop the fat-speak. Those belittling statements to yourself about your body will corrode your confidence.

All of us, no matter what size, need to spend the money and effort to dress well. Shopping can be intimidating; everything from the bright lights, three way mirrors and the thin mannequins leave us feeling less than confident. Some clothes make us look slightly larger, some slightly smaller. Truth is, we will always look approximately as fat as we are. No outfit can make you look 20 pounds thinner.

Focus on good fit even if it seems counter-intuitive that showing off our shape is the way to go. I have days when all I want to do is hide in my big and boxy, five-year-old ratty sweater. I don't leave the house. Over-sized garments only work for the waif-like 20-year-olds. For the rest of us, it leaves our figures undefined and as a result we look heavier than we actually are — and schlumpy too.

Wear fitted, not tight. Accentuate your assets and express your individuality. Accepting yourself frees up your energy to focus on the joy, pleasure and fun in your life.

Never judge your worth by your weight or let those pounds weigh you down.

don't label yourself

Age and size are only numbers. It's the attitude you bring to the clothes that makes the difference.

~Donna Karan

Your body is a shape, not a size. After all what is a size? It's nothing more than a general guideline used by manufacturers to help you to choose clothing that might fit you. So, before you berate yourself for not fitting into a certain size, know that a study published in *Clothing & Textiles* found that within a single size the waist measurement varied as much as eight and one-half inches across different brands.

The challenge: Each body is unique; long in places, short in places, curvy in places and straight in places. The fit of each manufacturer is also unique because each design house uses its own standards for its interpretation of average.

When a designer is creating a line of clothes, he uses a real person called a "fit" model. If the original pattern was drafted to the shape of a woman whose body is different from yours, that clothing is NEVER going to fit you. You simply need to keep trying on different clothing lines to find the fit that is closest to your body shape.

And, isn't it silly that we keep trying to squeeze ourselves into clothing that is a smaller size because we just don't believe that bigger is better? In fact, it is. Wearing a bigger size, makes you look smaller. If you are a small woman, wearing big clothes makes you look even smaller. Huh?

The majority of mature-bodied women wear clothes in size 12, 14 and 16 and seem to go through a considerable amount of angst when Misses sizing no longer gives them the ease and comfort they need and 14W, 16W and 18W is starting to fit better. Women's sizing simply means that a garment is cut a little fuller in the areas of the body where women naturally have curves.

Sometimes, depending upon the shape of your body, you may wear a Misses size 14 on top and Women's size 14 on the bottom, or vice versa, or any number of combinations. Nothing is right or wrong — it just is.

You probably have a size range in your closet at this very moment, all garments that fit you but made by different manufacturers. What size are you really? Who cares? If you do, take scissors to those size labels and enjoy a wardrobe that is perfectly fitted to you.

Stop obsessing about size and blaming your body for something that doesn't fit you properly. If you must lay blame, put it on the garment that wasn't cut for you to begin with.

Sometimes size *does* matter. No one wants a small glass of wine.

search for something new

If shopping doesn't make you happy, then you're in the wrong shop.

~Mimosa Rose

I don't like shopping. I like buying. It's not about the hunting it's about the gathering. In my many years in the fashion industry I was both a professional buyer and a professional shopper. I got paid to shop.

As a boutique owner, I made bi-annual trips to Montreal, Vancouver, Toronto and New York to buy seasonal inventory, timing the deliveries to ensure that there was always fresh product arriving. To the average shopper, the thought of flying off to New York sounds enticing; in fact, my days were quite gruelling. New York was not all bagels and Broadway. My days started early and ended late. Working months and months in advance I would make appointments with manufacturers and suppliers and in their showrooms, start sorting through the lines. Collections are made up of many different pieces. I would evaluate them based on fabric, line, shape, silhouette and value, bearing my clients pocketbooks in mind. It wasn't about my personal taste; I bought with the commercial knowledge of what sells, what works, what doesn't. On average, for every garment purchased, I would reject 40 or more. By the end of each buying trip everything started to look the same.

When I left the retail world to work as a consultant I was a personal shopper for my clients. I had no loyalty to any particular store and looked everywhere to find the perfect clothes for them.

These days I shop only for myself and I can assure you that I don't think there is anything recreational about retail shopping. My idea of a good time isn't trudging around a mall where you can't find a parking spot and have to fight crowds of people only to end up seeing the same stuff in store after store. I do appreciate the small independent retailers that offer unique labels and great service, but they don't always have the selection or sizes. Truth be told, I'm a Winners and Marshall's gal at heart even though it is the most hit and miss of all because I never know what they will have in until I get there. But that's half the fun.

I also love outlet malls. Who doesn't? But, before you drop your hard-earned cash let me explain how they operate. The purpose of outlet malls is mostly to liquidate manufacturers' overruns, discontinued designs, cancelled retail orders, damaged merchandise, incorrectly sized merchandise and one-of-a-kind designer samples. Just because you are in an outlet mall don't assume you are in an outlet store. Usually only about half the stores are true factory discount places.

And never assume that you will find the best bargain even if you are in an outlet store. Sometimes you can actually find an item cheaper when it is on sale in a regular store.

Tags that say "Compare at" aren't the same as SALE PRICE. It is a legal term that manufacturers use strictly for outlet stores. It also may be that it was manufactured specifically for an outlet store and, even though it may be brand name, it's not the same product that you would get in their regular stores. It's not a knock-off, it's the real deal, but the quality may be inferior. Does that matter? Maybe not.

The reality is that you can't find everything in one type of store. I end up buying in department stores, chain stores, specialty boutiques and discount stores — whichever type of store has what

I want and need at a price I am willing to pay. I like to save but sometimes paying full price is still worth the cash and is the best value.

That means looking everywhere at every price point. And that's work.

So, before you head out to indulge in some retail therapy remember this: Any item that is hanging in your closet that you are not wearing because it's not quite right for you is expensive no matter how deeply discounted it was when you bought it.

Whether you are on a tight budget, or have money to burn, before you take that item to the till ask yourself these questions:

- Is it a good color for me?

- Does the style of the garment suit me?

- Does it fit me now?

- Am I happy with the quality?

- Do I need this?

- Is it going to work well with what I already have?

- Do I feel great when I put it on?

- Why am I shopping?

Are you hungry for something new? Bored? Do you want to feel better about yourself? You might be looking for more than just clothing. Searching for something new is often the start of the process of internal reinvention too. For many, stores are the promised land of possibility.

I do feel a need to be completely candid about my bouts with recreational retail these days. I am a chronic roam-through-the-aisles person to see if I can find a deal on things I don't actually need — but — it might be a bargain too hard to resist, like on the third markdown. I try hard not to think with my sale brain (that's the one I use when I lose all reason about why I should not buy it). Logically I know that getting caught up in pursuit of the almighty bargain, and buying an item mostly because the store is practically giving it away, is just wrong.

If I do end up buying something truly special on sale, OMG I enjoy a tremendous sense of pride and accomplishment along with the bragging rights on my shopping savvy.

Then when someone tells me how much they like the great skirt I am wearing, I caress the fabric, smile, and in a proud manner herald "Twenty bucks. Winners."

Ultimately, we need to ask ourselves: How much will more clothing add to our happiness?

 But if you can't stop thinking about it … BUY IT.

uncover your secret strength

It's not about seducing men, it's about embracing womanhood.

~Dita Von Teese

My granddaughter Zoë, just two and recently potty trained, started to hop around at the mall as if she was dancing on a bed of hot coals. I took this as a sign that she had to go so I whisked her into the nearest public washroom. She made it. Yay!

I praised her, told her how proud I was of her, that she was a big girl now and didn't need to wear pull-ups anymore. With a huge smile on her face, and with a clear sense of accomplishment, she became quite excited and animated when she told me that she has lots of nice panties — her favorites being her purple Dora panties. Now we all know it's common to talk pee-pee and poo-poo in public with young children. So it wasn't surprising that at exactly the moment we were leaving the washroom, at exactly the moment we were walking past a line-up at the check-out, in all innocence she used her outside voice and asked: "What color *is* your panties Grandma?" Everyone chuckled. I blushed and made certain I didn't make eye contact with anyone. I leaned over and whispered to her sweet little face "My red ones honey and please use your inside voice."

Some days I wear my *Bridget Jones* proper panties. Other days call for my power panties. Not those provocative wisps we think we should wear for our partner — but those we wear for ourselves to celebrate growing out of girlhood and into a woman.

Let me tell you about mine.

After my second divorce my confidence and self-esteem was suffering. I felt fractured. I had always loved the color red but at that time in my life I wasn't emotionally ready to own the power that red represents — strength, courage, power and passion. I couldn't relate. It made me uncomfortable. So I didn't wear it.

But I had a little secret. Whenever I needed a psychological boost I would wear a pair of red panties. Not outside my clothes like a super-hero. My red (not so tiny) knickers were my hidden superpower. Wearing them made me feel invincible.

As I started to own my power, and my life again, I started to incorporate more red: first nail polish then handbags and shoes and ultimately apparel. Bringing red back into my being was a sure-fire confidence booster that made me feel vibrant and full of life.

That episode with Zoë prompted me that maybe my panties might not be as pretty as they once were. So, since then I've ruthlessly sorted through my pile of unmentionables and tossed any that were not up to snuff. Too old? Worn out? Lost their shape? Out they went.

On those days when I need to stand a little taller and be a little braver I still reach for my red reminders when I get dressed. After all, even a little girl knows that it feels nice to wear pretty panties.

know you are deserving

Do something today that you think is too delicious, too selfish, too wacky to fit within the rules of your life.

~Martha Beck

Although I was once obsessed with wearing the latest in designer labels, I have re-thought my priorities. So, what now? I've been there, done that for most styles and trends. The latest *it* items and fashion-forward pronouncements are no longer important to me. Don't get me wrong, I still love the fun and freshness of good fashion and staying current is fundamental. So, I've come to the conclusion that the best balance between the two is a less-is-more approach. That suits my sensibilities best.

When I go into a store, most often I am looking for something specific. But, sometimes going shopping doesn't turn out the way I expect. Like the time I intended to buy new underwear and ended up with a cashmere coat.

I know that as consumers we buy non-essentials because of emotion and then justify the purchase to ourselves with logic. The only *why* I could come up with for this purchase was that when I tried it on, I felt beautiful.

That's reason enough.

wear your life well

lessons from the journey

make room for a new you

recognize your value

claim your confidence

stay true to yourself

learn to say NO

reveal your true colors

live a colorful life

walk on the wild side

love what you've got

treat yourself gently

don't label yourself

search for something new

uncover your secret strength

know you are deserving

Download bonus *wear your life well* content at
www.wearyourlifewell.com

wear your life well

wear your life well

forgive yourself

The first step to truly living a good and fearless life is accepting responsibility for your actions. Accepting what part you had in any situation. Difficult, to say the least, but liberating.

~Jann Arden

In high school, I was voted "Most Likely to Get Married First" by my girlfriends. They were right. I bought into the "marriage is the ultimate life goal story." I married for the first time when I was only 18, just six months after graduation. I didn't have to, I wanted to. It was puppy love. Playing house seemed like a good idea. Maybe it was because I grew up without a father and so desperately wanted what (at the time) I thought would be a real family. Even though he was four years older and a college graduate we were both still kids. I thought my first marriage would be my only marriage, but it started to fall apart shortly after the wedding. We still had a lot of growing up to do. But, people don't always grow in the same direction and, when we realized that we didn't actually have a lot in common except the love we shared for our two children, we divorced after only four years. It was amicable as far as divorces go, but not without the inevitable sadness, anxiety and hurt. Just because the divorce was final it wasn't the end. We had kids, Christopher, three, and Lisa, only a year old.

I didn't go to college or university and I needed to support my children. I always had been a fast typist so I found a secretarial job. After all, that is what most women did back then.

When most of my friends were getting married for the first time I married my second husband. He was charismatic, charming and convincing. He swept me off my feet because I still had a basic belief that men always save women. I thought I was marrying the man of my dreams. While it all looks good to others, what happens behind the closed doors of a marriage is generally kept strictly secret. I didn't tell anyone that it became clear to me shortly after we were married that he had mental health problems. Divorce was not an option until it became the only option. He became possessive and abusive. He bullied me and berated me. He was unfaithful. The more he mistreated me the harder I tried to be perfect so that I would be lovable. That didn't work. I desperately wanted to get out but I didn't know how. I was too embarrassed to let people know what was really going on so I played at being happily married for 12 years. Over that time, he demoralized me. I felt worthless. I felt shame. I was scared. Eleanor Roosevelt once said, "No one can make you feel inferior without your consent." That thought played over and over in my head and I knew that I had to stand up for myself and say "enough." He threatened to kill me if I ever left him and he slept with a loaded handgun under the mattress to remind me. I had no money and I didn't know what would happen next if I did leave. I had two children who depended upon me.

I stopped pretending my life was perfect, even though I wanted it to be. Choosing whether to walk away or whether to try harder was a hard decision. I found my inner power and the strength to leave him — restraining order and all. That marriage taught me a lot — mostly what I didn't want in a relationship. The divorce proceedings were painful and I chose to walk away with nothing but my self-respect. That was the one thing he could not take from me.

There is nothing easy about getting a divorce and judgement from otherwise well-meaning friends and family only makes it worse. Divorce is anything but the easy way out and making the decision was life-altering. People were disappointed in me. A broken marriage was a secret to hide away, a stigma, a mark of real failure. I'd had two. It felt like another death to me only this time without a funeral — and it was hope that died.

Notwithstanding the pain and the shame, I fell in love again. He was an alcoholic so that didn't work out well either. I had been on three emotional roller coasters before I went into the unfamiliar territory of a being a single woman with a broken heart. One minute I was happy, the next I would become angry, then sad. I felt alone. Sometimes I felt like I was straight-up crazy. I dated a bit but the hurt-little-girl part of me believed that I didn't deserve to be loved. After all, what did I have to offer? Who would ever love me? I was a failure. I didn't think I could ever trust anyone again. Especially myself. What if I failed again? I told myself I was done with dating. I didn't care anymore. I was fine being by myself with my two kids, now grown.

The universe was not exactly short on wake-up calls and soon I realized there was something else that I needed to do. I finally tuned into the lesson. My history was proof that to heal outside you must heal inside first. Now that I was alone I needed to learn to love and cherish myself. That discovery was a journey in itself.

I was holding onto a grudge and the idea of forgiveness seemed impossible, yet letting go of the feeling of being "wronged" just didn't seem right either. Deep down I recognized that the hurt had not yet healed because I had not let it. By holding onto the negative emotion, I left myself vulnerable – left myself open to being hurt again

I decided that instead of wallowing in the past pain, I would make a choice to live from empowerment, not victimhood. I needed to move on from my mis-steps. After all, my mistakes allowed me to confront what I truly wanted out of life. I started to live each day for what it was — a new beginning. Divorce is devastating but it's also liberating. I finally felt emotionally safe again. As I let go of the stress and painful emotions I started to feel a new energy emerge as I took control of my life. I finally understood it was up to me to be my own best friend and to give myself the love and respect that I so desperately wanted. I vowed to never again choose to be with a man who didn't respect me. Finally, I forgave all three.

The time came where I had to stop beating myself up over the mistakes I made. I forgave myself for not knowing what I didn't know before I learned it. Even though the shame, regret and anxiety were not easily resolved, it felt so good to let them go. What was there to be ashamed of? I went through a rough time and I'm proud I got out of it alive. I felt like a new version of myself was waking up. I was happy, my self-esteem was healthy and my career was evolving. Great things started to happen when I gave as much energy to my dreams as I did to my fears. I learned that what looks like failure can actually be success.

At the age of 42, when I was least expecting it, I met the man who today cherishes me and has helped me to heal the wounds of my past.

Here is what I know is true: A relationship is not the main indicator of your happiness. I accept as true that Scottie showed up in my life because I did the emotional work I needed to do. I learned to depend on me.

The most important love is that which you give yourself.

find your voice

What makes you a feminist is not saying that you are feminist, it's in how you choose to live your life, what you do and the action that you take.

~Emma Watson

My mother grew up in war-torn Europe and suffered intolerances and injustice for no reason other than she was the wrong nationality and the wrong gender.

When she came to Canada with her husband in the 1950s she had never heard the word feminist. It's a 1960s word. Since English was her second language she sometimes searched for the word with the sort-of right meaning. It didn't always come out correctly, but I always knew what she meant. When I ponder it, the idea that feminism was created in the last 50 years is silly. Women have been powerful characters throughout history.

In our conversations, my mother told me she was never one of those women chauvinists or whatever you call them. She just believed that all women deserve to be treated as an equal human being instead of as a piece of property. The idea of being treated as valuable, of having similar opportunities, of being paid a fair wage and of not having her life dictated by someone just because she was born female was not a radical concept to her. Yet, inequality was her reality early on.

Tragically widowed when she was only 29 she knew that in order to move forward gender could not be part of the equation any longer. After all she now had the role of mother and father.

The problem was that gender identified and described how she should be, not how she was. Culture dictated a woman's place and made it acceptable for society to exclude and disrespect her despite her circumstances. She supported and raised her family dancing through her life "backwards and in high heels."

A quiet-spoken woman she was never comfortable in the spotlight. She didn't expound upon her feelings of the injustice between genders in a crowd. She explored them within herself because she believed that women had to tread lightly in order to change cultural history and to live peacefully. She did speak to me quietly as often as she could to teach me what she referred to as "just the fair thing."

I grew up in the 1960s and early 70s. It was a time when radical feminists were burning their bras, had hairy arm pits and lots of free sex as a result of the Pill. These revolutionaries raised hemlines and eyebrows. Furthermore, they were talking about scary empowering things to other women who were not ready to shake up the status quo. I was too young to be part of it, but watched in wonder as the word feminist became an "F" word. A lot of the backlash came from other women. Being called a feminist was not a compliment because many associated it with women who were man-haters or angry, bitter lesbians. Label them what you will, they were trailblazers.

Embracing the complexities of my heritage as a woman, I like to think of myself as a feminist, living in a time when my experience as a woman is primarily that of a human being. I choose not to be apologetic for my femaleness and femininity. And it is only possible because of the first feminists, the suffragettes of the pre-1920s, who asked for the right to vote and all those who, in the subsequent years, went on to make a statement about womanhood and what it should be.

We live in an extra-ordinary era where we can instantly and effortlessly connect with hundreds and even thousands of people at a time. Yet, it is not necessary to be on the "Most Influential Women in the World" list to make a difference.

For most of us, the most meaningful influence we have still remains one-on-one. We can influence our culture by raising our sons and daughters differently and speaking to anyone who will listen about what's just fair. What matters is our mind-set and what we believe and value about gender. Even in our western world today, there is still an inequity and we must fix it. Each generation wants something better for its daughters and feminism is still relevant.

With my mother's encouraging words resonating in my head, and the fact that I live in a time when societal standards are vastly different from those of yesteryear, I find still the need to challenge myself from time to time to unlearn some of the gender expectations and lessons that I internalized growing up.

I am thankful for the men and women whose passion and power for feminism resonates around the world in a loud voice, and, for those who like my mother influence quietly with their soft voices.

The word feminist is strong and succinct. It's a label that some people see as negative. What would we replace it with? Girl Power? Sisterhood? Quite frankly those are weak words and they just don't pay respect to the challenges, sacrifices and courage of those who carried the cause forward before us.

Today, we all have a bigger voice, more choices and more options than any other generation. It's time to change the conversation about what it means to be a feminist: to dust off this often-misunderstood word and re-empower it.

We are the ones to do it. Feminists have given us our voice.
It's time for us to use it.

make a difference

*The first step toward changing the world is to change our vision
of the world and of our place in it.*

~Arianna Huffington

I remember getting into the police car. My mom woke me when it
was still dark and told me that my brother and I were going to our
aunt's house. I always liked going there and playing with my
cousins, so I thought it would be a good thing. The police drove us
there and then took my mom away with them. When she left she
told me that it was all going to be okay; that she was going to see
my dad.

I was confused.

I didn't see her again for two days. She was crying when she told
me that my papa had gone to live with the angels. I didn't yet
understand that she meant it would be forever. What does a
seven-year-old know about death?

For a long time, I thought that he would walk through the door
again. He never did. I didn't even get to say good-bye. My loss was
almost unbearable. The defining change in my life was the death
of my father — it created broken places inside that altered me
forever. Growing up, I never knew the love and guidance a father
contributes to preparing his child for life.

And so, over the years, it has been women, my mother among
them, who have had the strongest influence on me. Some of them
I have known personally, others are public figures and some are
fictional characters. The thing they all have in common is the

lasting impression they have made on me because of the inspiring attributes they embody.

My first fictional female hero was very real to me. In elementary school if I got good grades I got a Nancy Drew mystery as a reward. The first one I ever read was *The Bungalow Mystery* and over the years I read all the variations of solving mysteries and restoring social order in *The Clue in the Diary*, *The Secret in the Old Attic*, *The Hidden Staircase* and many other stories of her adventures. I was mesmerized by the words on each page and I'm sure I read every book at least twice. Nancy was cool, competent and curious. There was no mystery so baffling that she could not solve it. Her super sleuth skills were even more amazing to me because she had a mind of her own and didn't believe that she was limited just because she was a girl. She could climb a fence like a boy and yet prove to us that it is fantastic and amazing to be a girl.

Nancy Drew's favorite color was blue. Mine too. She had blonde hair and blue eyes. Me too. The fact that she had only one parent (her mother died when she was three years old) implied an uncommon bond between us. I imagined I was one of her best friends and went on adventures with her alongside her girlfriends Bess and George. I dreamed that someday I, too, would have a handsome and adoring boyfriend like Ned Nickerson.

Nancy Drew helped me to understand that you can be smart and not have to hide it. She is all grown up now. This year she turns 85. I will always think of her as the formative "girl power"' icon in my life.

Wonder Woman was my favorite comic book character. She was the warrior princess who had superhuman powers and who fought for justice, love, peace and gender equality.

There are so many women who were female firsts throughout history. They have broken records, broken ground and suffered trials. They were both brave and bold. In our modern world, my list of exceptional women continues to grow. They are the peacekeepers, storytellers, activists, leaders, healers and artists who are actively engaged in making our world a better place. I spend a lot of time thinking about how I can be more like them. They are doing great things — even world-changing things. Their stories dare me to ponder what I want to accomplish and why.

Amelia Earhart was a pioneer in aviation, wrote best-selling books and designed her own clothes. The way I see it, I have important things to say and do AND I can make my mark on the world while wearing beautiful clothes.

wear your life well

cherish your mother

I realized when you look at your mother, you are looking at the purest love you will ever know.

~Mitch Albom

The mother/daughter bond is complex and it changes with each stage of life. Over the passage of time, from childhood to adulthood, the emotional bonds of intimacy and vulnerability are being established. Whether our relationships are loving, fragile, fraught with conflict — or a synthesis of all of these — our mothers have helped to make us who we are today. During the lifetime we share we come to a mature acceptance and understanding and an immense gratitude for the impact we have on each other.

I had one of those moments, the I-just-didn't-realize instant when my relationship with my mother forever expanded.

In preparation for her 80th birthday celebration I'd gathered old photographs, talked with friends and family members and listened to lots of stories in order to try to capture her essence and her life.

Sounds simple enough but it wasn't easy. Despite all the different hairdos, outfits, looks and sizes over the years, I really had only one picture of her in my mind but there was an *aha* moment when I realized that she has played many roles to many people in her life — that she is much more than just my mother.

As fate would have it my mother had to go it alone because death took my father out of the picture. Like her mother before her she was left to support my brother and me on her own while she struggled with the realities of the full spectrum of life. There was no woman's work; it was all work that had to be done and since she was both breadwinner and nurturer she worked hard. *Extremely* hard. I never heard her complain about it but sometimes at night, when she was in bed, I could hear her crying softly as she struggled to sleep. She wanted to stay strong in front of us. Her belief was she would do what she had to do to keep us together. That was the immigrant mentality she was raised with and the values that carried her through the toughest of times.

She didn't know what lay in store for us so, with two young children, she took control of her fate and did boldly what she knew how to do. There was no option. As a woman who didn't know how to read or write English she supplemented her meager monthly Workman's Compensation pension by caring for children during the day and sewing for clients at night, all so she could remain at home to care for us. She was a proud and dignified woman and never took a hand-out or a dime from anyone. She just figured it out *somehow*. We never went hungry and we were always well-dressed and well-loved.

Like most mother/daughter relationships over the years, we have consistently loved each other and driven each other crazy at the same time. We've always worked things out and been there for one another. I haven't always told her how much I appreciate her because, quite frankly, I spent too much time being her child while around her. So, it's about time that I share some heartfelt sentiments.

Dear Mom,

I admire your strength. You've had a difficult life and yet remain one of the most resilient people I know.

I admire your love and acceptance. You love everyone for exactly who they are and make extraordinary efforts to make sure your love is felt.

I admire how well you take care of yourself. You know how important it is to stay healthy in order to maintain quality of life.

I admire what a wonderful friend you are. You are always there for people with kind words or a listening ear to support those who need it.

I admire how much everyone loves you.

You taught me by example how to be patient and kind. You value my opinions and encourage me to express myself honestly. You always make me feel special because you appreciate my strengths.

I really do want to be just like you Mom. I'm starting to have the same facial expressions as you. Some of my habits are strangely similar to yours now. I know my Christmas cookies will never taste as good and I'll admit that I've given my children every piece of advice you've given me, even though I rejected it at the time.

I try, Mom. I try.

You are a wonderful mother and friend. I'm glad you are mine.

I love you.

Helene

wear your life well

embrace your evolution

I think that playing dress-up begins at age five and never truly ends.

~Kate Spade

Maiden. Mother. Crone. These are the three stages of a woman's life found in the mythology of feminine wisdom in various European cultures. This archetypical triad has traditionally represented the functions and focuses of each life stage as our hormonal shifts demarcate them. Over the course of longer and longer lives our fashion choice and personal style evolve gradually as well.

The *maiden* represents new beginnings, playfulness, spontaneity and learning. Think back. In our teens and 20s we were going to school, having adventures, getting our first jobs and finding our first love. We were busy playing dress-up and the fashion world (and stores) catered to us. Comfortable experimenting with a lot of different looks, we were looking for our identity through clothes. It was a time in our lives when we didn't have a lot of responsibility, we wanted it all and we wanted it all at the same time.

In our 30s and 40s we moved into the second stage of our life living under the ethos of *mother* whether or not we had biological children. Our intrinsic worth was fertility, stability and strength. We established our identities through the roles we played in our relationships with our kids and in our career: grown-up things like finding our potential soul mates, joining the mommy club and struggling to find balance in our lives as we ran on empty. Paying off student loans, disbursing funds for daycare, meeting mortgage payments, and all the other responsibilities that came with this time of life, often meant that the amount of time, money and energy we had to spend on ourselves was restricted and also less of a priority. We still looked pretty good even though life was a lot more complex.

Finally, by the time we reach our 50s and 60s, we have outgrown much of who we were and with the help of menopause most of our clothing as well. No longer young, but far from old, it's the time in life when we might start feeling lost, not really sure of who we are or what to wear anymore. Even though we may be grandmothers (and loving it) we don't want to wear *grandma* clothes and the things that used to work well might not anymore. Our roles and identities are changing once again and our closets often reflect it. We have more time, more money and more courage to come to grips with aging plus the opportunity to embrace the potential of all our possibilities. In ancient culture this stage was known as the *crone* — the old woman who holds all the wisdom of the journeys of womanhood within her.

Whoa.

Go ahead. Say the word out loud.

Crone.

What an awful sounding word. It offends me. It makes me think of a cantankerous hag, a nasty, malicious and withered, witchy-looking woman.

I would rather be called a witch than a crone. It's true that the Wicked Witch of the West is old and ugly, but I would choose to identify with glamorous Glinda, the Good Witch of the North.

It is thought that, as a noun, crone entered the English language around the year 1390, derived from the Anglo-French word carogne, caroigne, meaning a disagreeable woman. So why is it that today the word crone has become a synonym for an old and wise woman?

I aspire to become a modern-day wise woman who is full of fun, vigor and vitality. A woman with stories, life experiences, sass and style. I will embrace the grace, dignity and beauty that comes with age because I am happier and more in-tune with myself than ever before.

But please, don't ever call me a crone.

Try *wicked*.

wear your life well

get playful

It is a happy talent to know how to play.

~Ralph Waldo Emerson

Once we reach adulthood it's time to get serious. Right? You know — all work and no play. But who decided that we don't need novelty and pleasure when we grow up — those purposeless, fun and pleasurable moments that increase our joy and enrich our connectedness and creativity. Simply "adulting" doesn't make us happy. For that we need to give ourselves permission to play — everyday.

My mom is a Virgo. She is German. Being practical is part of her DNA. The very notion of taking time for herself is foreign. As a young widow her only social circle and support was from family, the church ladies and a handful of close friends.

Fun. What's that? Even if she did manage to find a few extra minutes in her day she would simply find more things to do for others. Culturally women are expected to take care of everyone else and forgo their own needs. For my mom, the very idea of going out and doing things *just for fun*, and without a man by her side, was not even considered. Decades ago the notion of women having a good time independent of their roles as wives and mothers was not accepted. Society would have labelled them selfish. Women were expected to be tied to the home. In keeping with expectations my mother didn't date and marry again until she had launched her youngest child.

I invited my mother to come with me to the very first *Ultimate Pajama Party*®. It was a big decision for her. She reminded me that she had never, ever, been away on any kind of trip unless it was with her husband or on a family vacation. Her life was so routine that she couldn't even remember the last time she had done something for the first time.

It was apparent that she had tremendous guilt over even considering my invitation. Gradually, then excitedly, she decided to come.

She had the time of her life. The guilt was gone.

Several months later I was invited to speak at a Mother/Daughter Spa event at the Fairmont Banff Springs Hotel. Naturally I invited my mom.

Evidently she decided to add an element of impracticality and indulgence to her life.

She went shopping and bought new luggage.

find your funny

Life is too important to be taken seriously.

~Oscar Wilde

The first time it happened I was horrified.

Within a few days of my 55th birthday, I stopped at a corner drug store to pick up some cleaning supplies on my way to my son's condo. He had just moved out and I was going over to help him give it a thorough cleaning before the new owners took possession. I'll admit I wasn't exactly looking my best.

As I was paying for the paper towels the cashier invited me to their upcoming Seniors' Appreciation Day. To add insult to injury she went on to explain that I didn't need to purchase anything in order to enjoy the free coffee and donuts. Now, I might have forgiven her if she was some young 'un behind the counter with a basic belief that anyone over 30 is old. But that wasn't the case. If the clerk had asked me the question I could have lied. Instead she simply assumed it. I wanted to feign indignation, but resisted.

It happened again that summer at the local garden center. Apparently, Tuesdays are Seniors' Days and us old folks (does that really include me?) can enjoy 10 per cent off any purchases. When asked if I was a senior, I told her I would use my Horticultural Club membership card to qualify for the same discount. Obviously, I was still in denial.

The next time I was back in the drug store I was more dressed up and looking to buy some new cosmetics. The loose mineral powder I was planning to purchase cost $49 and the lovely mature woman behind the counter told me that if I spent $50 that day I would be entitled to a 20 percent senior's discount. That's all the convincing that I needed because the next thing you know I was looking for a lip gloss. The problem was that the writing on the bottom of the tube was so small I couldn't read it. Within moments three menopausal mamas' (myself, the store clerk and the woman who happened to be standing near me at the counter) all had on our reading glasses trying to see if that teeny, tiny text said *Exotic Orchid*.

As if on cue, we three strangers looked at each other and our smiles suddenly burst into giggles followed by unadulterated, goofy laughter. All of a sudden, we were a sisterhood.

I'm okay with it all now. If I don't get asked "are you a senior citizen, ma'am?" I make sure I let them know that I am. After all my mother always told me that a "penny saved is a penny earned." Now, I'm looking forward to my monthly seniors' stipend.

Lighten up. Laugh at yourself. Find things to smile about as you consciously tune into the lighthearted and uplifting moments in life. It makes your body feel happy and your heart sing.

get over getting older

We have to value ourselves not for what we look like or the things we possess but for the women we are.

~Maya Angelou

Most of the time I like being the age I am, but this aging stuff is complex. Inside I still feel like I'm in my 30s, but then I realize my children are over 40. I recently caught a glimpse of my hands and became aware of the fact that they look like my mother's. Sometimes when I pass a mirror I'm still surprised that I don't see a younger woman anymore. I'm trying to make peace with the lines around my eyes and brackets around my mouth, justifying them with the fact that I laugh a lot. But saggy skin on my hands and arms — yikes.

Although easier said than done, there is no point in having angst about aging. I will get old. I might be fat or thin. Some days I will look radiant and others dragged-out and worn-down.

"Our concern with how we look as we age may be superficial, but it's natural. We shouldn't be ashamed of obsessing about it from time to time. After all, this is one aspect of the passage to the Age of Mastery that all of us face," writes Gail Sheehy in *New Passages*. "It's about finding a new version of attractiveness. It's making the most of whatever external beauty we have, but also activating sources of internal value. Once we begin to accept and enjoy the roundedness and normal weight gain, the wrinkles and sags that come naturally with maturity, we become grounded. And being grounded, we can build on the two pillars that make

147

the new older woman such good value; her complexity and her uniqueness."

Like every other woman, I can't stop or reverse the aging process no matter what I do or how well I take care of myself. No matter how much I exercise, how many hours I sleep or how healthy I eat, I'm still aging. I don't have a best-before date and no matter what the cosmetic companies claim, a jar of expensive face cream doesn't contain the fountain of youth. I have made the decision that Botox and cosmetic surgery is not for me because I believe that the best face to put forward to the world is the one I was born with.

I like me. I have a happy life. I've finally figured out who and what I want to be when I grow up and there is still so much more that I want to do. And so be it that if, along with these gifts of life, the other "joyful" aspects of aging materialize — like chin hairs, sagging skin, a slipping memory, age spots and an ever-expanding waistline.

I'll never really figure everything out, but there is a sense that as I get older I know more. After all, my life has given me lots of experiences, memories and even scars to draw upon. Hopefully, by now, I have the wisdom to reflect upon what I have experienced and have sorted out what is really important to me — things like staying productive and creative, learning new things, seeing new places, having fun, living authentically and passing along what I have learned to the generation that follows me.

There is a lot about aging that scares me. I won't pretend otherwise. Yet, I know aging is not only about decline, but also about growth and possibility.

I do know that when I look my personal best I feel personally powerful. When I feel personally powerful I believe in myself and choose to embrace life no matter what challenging times and incredible opportunities await me.

So, instead of having a vanity crisis I've decided to embrace the journey into my next life cycle.

I choose to love who I am today. That is what will help me deal with whatever comes tomorrow.

wear your life well

be your own hero

Age to women is like Kryptonite to Superman.

~Kathy Lette

The *Invisible Woman* is a fictional character, a Marvel Comics super heroine and the soul of the *Fantastic Four*. She plays a vital role in the lives of her family, her husband, her children and her friends. She has the ability to project powerful fields of energy and render herself invisible.

Like the Marvel heroine, younger women are seen and valued for their beauty and energy while older women are admired for their wisdom and character. But in the eyes of a youth-fixated culture, a woman who is no longer young and who is afraid to accept the vulnerability age brings enters *The Invisible Age* — a time of feeling unimportant and unnoticed, all of which come at a time when there are not only physical changes but hormonal and emotional roller coasters as well. Is it any wonder that women struggle to redefine themselves during this time of transition?

The thing to remember is that a woman remains invisible by choice. She can allow society to perceive her as a one-dimensional woman: middle-aged, middle-class and middle-of-the-road. Or, she can claim her personal power and become her own heroine by refusing to let a myth sap her perception of herself or her joy.

When you look at yourself who do you see?

A woman who is ready to conquer the world?

No?

Remember if you don't believe in your power others won't either. Let's ensure that the *Visible Woman* is not a fictional character but instead a real-life genuine super heroine.

You.

You've got this.

grow through life

And the day came when the risk to remain tight in a bud was more painful than the risk it took to blossom.

~Anais Nin

I love to play in the dirt. Living where I do the season is short and that makes each gardening day even more precious. My garden is the quiet place where I can think without all the continuous distractions in life. I can spend hours and hours on end digging, transplanting, hoeing and hauling.

My garden gives me the simple joy of being in touch with nature and myself. The scene changes as it shifts and grows. It's never done. As the different plants show their gifts throughout the season I see the personality and uniqueness of each. Sometimes I have to prune and replant, other times just water and fertilize. Year after year I appreciate the ever-changing aspects it expresses to me.

When I was a young girl I would go to my grandmother's farm where she taught me about growing a garden. My Oma always had such beautiful flowers and I know that my love of any variety is the result, unequivocally, of my early exposure to watching her cultivate with care and appreciation, the unique potential in every blossom.

I always felt important when she let me help irrigate her dry-land, market-sized vegetable garden. It wasn't just a hobby for her. It was survival. It provided food for the winter months ahead. We would form strategically placed trenches with a hoe so that the water (which had to be hauled in by truck) could find its way to the roots. Of course, the reward for all of this hard work was the shared sense of achievement we enjoyed with each other and the fresh vegetables harvested.

I simply don't want to go through life, I intend to grow through life. My garden has become a metaphor; it takes a lifetime to produce my fullest potential. It illuminates for me that on-going learning, growing, changing and evolving is what keeps me interesting and interested.

When you value personal growth your sense of pleasure and satisfaction gives you self-confidence; and that can make all the difference in cultivating the real you.

Live your life in full bloom.

never give up

For a tree to become tall it must grow tough roots among the rocks.

~Friedrich Nietzsche

Paralyzed by the fear of reviving the pain of her past, my mother guarded the secrets of her life as a young woman. For 75 years, this story has remained hidden — and heavy in her heart.

She doesn't speak of them often. They were not the good ol' days.

My mother Elise, until she was 10 years old, lived with the simple joy of being young. She was one of six children in a family that was both well-to-do and respected in the community. Her parents owned a large home and a substantial parcel of land in the town of Mramorak in the Danube Valley that included a vineyard, orchard and farmland. They were *Volksdeutsche* — people of ethnic German descent who had been living in the Banat region of Yugoslavia for many generations.

My mother was in Fourth Grade when Yugoslavia fell to Nazi Germany in 1941. All the men were called to war and if they refused they were shot. There were no female teachers at that time. The school was shut down. Education was now an impossible dream.

Her father Christian went to war. They never saw him again. Her oldest brother Philip, barely 16, was also at war. Her mother Elisabeth bore the responsibility of rearing the family. One day she enlisted help from her two oldest daughters — 10-year-old

Elise and 12-year-old Margarete. They were to keep the house clean, cook the meals, wash the clothes and tend to the livestock. Elisabeth went to work from dawn to dusk alongside other laborers. Her five youngest including eight-year-old Peter, four-year-old Carl and Helene, just two, were left to fend for themselves. They all did what they had to do.

By the time German troops withdrew in the autumn of 1944 the Resistance Movement in Yugoslavia, led by Josef Tito, was in full control. He and his Partisans took revenge where they could. Their crimes would come to be known as the German Genocide. All legal rights including citizenship were cancelled for at least 195,000 German-speaking citizens. General Tito's followers exterminated 10s of thousands of men, women and children living in this region.

My mother — now 13 — was one of the lucky ones. During nights that were rampant with rape Elisabeth hid Elise and Margarete in a large pit covered with straw. They would often spend the entire night buried until the screams subsided and the only sound was silence.

The men in the community were either tortured, shot or beaten to death. My mother's Uncle Michel and his five sons were forced to dig a mass grave so that the Partisans could use their bodies for target practice.

General Tito had a heinous execution in mind on October 20, 1944. Partisans beat the drums on every street corner while his troops terrorized my mother, her family and hundreds of other women and children as they were herded into the central town square. The German women and children saw barrels filled with gasoline and understood that the intent was to burn them alive. Without intervention they were helpless.

The Russians — despite their reputation for being ruthless — came to the rescue preventing that particular horror and protecting my mother and others from an inferno.

The Red Army had reached Yugoslavia just weeks before. Leaders had been directed to establish Yugoslavia as a Communist Soviet Bloc country and to challenge Tito's leadership.

In the middle of the night in April, 1945, the Partisans drove Elisabeth, her aging mother and her five children out of their home. Everything was taken; they were allowed only the clothes on the chair beside their beds. That clothing would be all they would wear for the next three years. They never again saw their home.

They were moved into one of eight prison camps built for those who were unable to work — the old, the sick, mothers and small children. Each was given a spot on a hay-covered floor and one blanket. There were no beds and no pillows. Rats were everywhere. There was no soap, no salt, no bread and the only meat they had was obtained when horses died of starvation. Their primary diet was gruel in the morning and bean soup thick with dead flies at day's end.

My mother's brother Peter, then 13, was beaten and left for dead because he was so hungry he had stolen cherries from a tree. Fresh fruit was only for the Yugoslavs. When he regained consciousness the next day, his ribs broken and his face almost unrecognizable, he pulled himself along the ground and made his way home.

The camp had 30,000 prisoners and thousands of women and children were raped, beaten, tortured and shot. More than 100 people died each day. My mother saw her grandmother's lifeless body being wrapped in burlap and tossed onto a horse-drawn disposal wagon with the other dead-of-the-day. She watched as her mother Elisabeth ran beside that wagon beseeching and begging that they would not remove her mother's clothing. She prayed they would leave her with dignity in death.

Life was hard. But Elisabeth was smart. She had a plan. Her vision of leading her family to safety became greater than her fear. Her dream of their escape forced her to choose hope over despair.

In the depths of darkness, she and her children crept under the barbed-wire fence, crawling to prevent the bullets flying overhead from killing them. They slipped away to freedom and the unknown. They made their way across Europe starting with a walk across Hungary. They were cold. They had neither food nor money.

It was autumn and the local farmers were harvesting field corn. They would cut the cornstalks close to the ground, gather them by hand and stack them teepee-style until they were dry enough to be stored. The corn shocks provided perfect hiding places during the day. When night fell, the family would continue walking away from all they knew. They would stop at local churches and relied on the kindness of strangers for food.

In Austria, a local family took them in briefly to get them ready to return to Germany. They were given some food and a little money. The rest of the journey was by train — as stowaways.

In Germany, they were taken to a quarantine facility in Ludwigsburg where they were deloused, fed, given new clothes and medical care. After that, they found home in a military barracks at an abandoned airfield-turned-refugee-camp in Malmsheim near Stuttgart. They, along with hundreds of other displaced Germans known as the *Heimatvertriebene,* found relief, safety and the opportunity to rebuild their lives. Now 17, my mother had a proper bed and pillow. She went to work in a factory, learned her trade as a seamstress and started a new life.

Elisabeth found a two-room apartment for the family of six. Philip had survived the war and was reunited with the rest. One day he brought a friend home. That friend, Ernst, would become my father. Ernst and Elise married a year later and he moved in too.

Their first-born, a son also named Ernst, died within days due to a heart defect.

In 1950 when my grandmother Elisabeth and the rest of the family immigrated to Canada my parents chose to stay in Germany. They lived with my father's family however there was little work in a country that was struggling to rebuild.

The luxury of having a choice about the kind of life they wanted to create was alluring. Deciding to focus on where they were going instead of what they had been through they joined the rest of the family in Canada a year later.

Their Atlantic passage was on the *SS Beaverbrae* and the ship was anything but a luxury cruise liner. They arrived in Halifax on a cold January morning to a warm reception of tea and sandwiches served by local women.

My parents didn't speak English or French. They had only $20. They travelled by train arriving in southern Alberta in the midst of a harsh prairie winter. The farmer who employed the rest of the family sponsored them too. As migrant field workers they were provided a shanty shack, potatoes and the opportunity to work.

Tragically widowed when she was only 29 my mother raised my brother and I on a pittance — sewing late into the night to make ends meet.

She hid her pain well. Only I saw the vulnerability in her face as she tucked me in at night. That was not the face she allowed the world to see.

My mother survived unimaginable circumstances with resolve and an indomitable spirit. She never abandoned her hopes and dreams.

Today, in her 80s, she takes a daily walk in the park enjoying the life she created for herself and the freedom to greet people with her gentle face, soft smile and kind words.

She still shows the world a brave face.

We can't know what anyone else has gone through or is experiencing currently. We can only take our own journey. I do know when things get hard I try to remember that the life I might complain about is only a dream for others. Each day I attempt to focus on at least one thing for which I am truly grateful. That helps me zero in on what more I may need or want. Life can make us bitter — or we can get better.

My mother's story was a different time and a different war. Any crisis in the human journey is not so dissimilar. Perhaps the past enters the present to illuminate that no matter what circumstances and obstacles we have overcome, or struggle with now, we are the author of our own life. Our choices don't belong to fate. They belong to us.

My mother's life has taught me never to limit the vision I have for myself based on my current circumstances.

We are all survivors somehow. If we look to the future and the good in life, we will always find it.

look for the treasures in life's scars

You may encounter many defeats, but you must not be defeated. In fact, it may be necessary to encounter the defeats, so that you can know who you are, what you can rise from, how you can still come out of it.

~Maya Angelou

Some of the worst moments of my life are what made me the strong woman I am today. Those lessons and challenges often left me feeling fatigued and confused and, at times, even fractured and broken. In those dark moments, I often questioned whether I had what it would take to pick up the pieces and put myself back together again.

In the late 15th Century a Shogun sent a prized and damaged tea bowl to be fixed. It came back held together with ugly metal staples. Voila, imperfection breeds perfection. The Japanese craftsmen were inspired to seek a new way to mend ceramics.

They developed a method called *Kintsugi*. The broken places were highlighted with a lacquer resin sprinkled with powdered gold. The Japanese believe that when something has suffered damage, and has a history, that once fixed it will look more gorgeous and be more precious than before it was fractured.

Collectors developed such a love for *Kintsugi* that some were accused of deliberately breaking prized ceramics so that they could be mended and enhanced with this distinctive Japanese technique.

Like the damaged tea bowl, I didn't welcome being broken or the unsought time in painful experiences. But they are part of what shaped my identity. Whether life thrusts something difficult at me or if I choose to try something challenging and scary I take the lessons I've learned and move forward. Each experience has helped me to learn, to grow and to take away a revelation, no matter the outcome. I have learned that change is constant and that there is no final destination in reinvention.

At some point life tries to break everyone. There always will be challenges and whether we make small tweaks to our lives, or shake things up in a major way, we have the opportunity to fill the seams with the gold of our life experiences.

In the end, I will only regret the chances I didn't take and the decisions I waited too long to make.

And the same holds true for you.

Be brave.

live like there's no tomorrow

A long life may not be good enough, but a good life is long enough.

~Benjamin Franklin

I've always been a person who didn't give in to every little ache and pain. My life is busy. I don't have time to be sick. I took pride in the fact that I hadn't seen a doctor for years, because, getting sick doesn't happen to *me*.

Until it did. Now, I was out of breath walking up a flight of stairs, that tickle in my throat became a chronic cough and swallowing became a challenge. I wasn't feeling up to participating in life and I was getting worse as time went on.

My physician asked me to trust a team of specialists who would take care of my health crisis and urged me to adopt a policy of *no Internet surfing*. Late on a night when I didn't heed his advice I finally *got it;* that a do-it-yourself diagnosis with Dr. Google isn't a good idea.

It was a terrible year. I had scopes, tests, scans, ultrasounds and biopsies. There were more questions than answers on this medical merry-go-round. My mind went to the worst-case scenarios. Death is something that we often don't talk about, or even think about, but I was scared and thought about it a lot. I was facing the fears and feeling the feelings while I was living in the unknown. In retrospect, I realize that thinking about death helped me to clarify my life.

I was expecting a bad diagnosis. As it turned out, the tumor was benign. No Cancer. And the disease in my body was not as sinister as I had imagined — chronic but manageable.

When I realized I was not dying I began to observe myself as a new person learning how to experience life again. I am changed. We often live as if we have all the time in the world. But, time is different now — it's more precious. I fully grasp that with a finite existence in this world I need to make the time to do what makes me happy.

It was about this time that I read about Candy Chang's "Before I die ..." wall in Austin, Texas — a participatory public art project that invites people to reflect on life, to contemplate death, and to share their personal aspirations. Now I have designated a "Before I die ..." page in my journal to encourage me to celebrate hope and possibility.

My dominant thought: "Am I living fully now?" I know that the answers to these "fill in the blanks" questions are more significant than those I was asked on any exam I took in school. It's comforting to know that there are no wrong responses. Yet, the answers don't mean a thing if I don't take action toward making them a reality.

Queen Latifah sings to my soul:

I'm gonna live till I die. I'm gonna laugh 'stead of cry. Before my number's up, I'm gonna fill my cup. I'm gonna live, live, live till I die.

Hallelujah, gonna dance, gonna fly, I'll take a chance riding high. Before my number's up, I'm gonna fill my cup. I'm gonna live, live, live, until I die.

So here is what my "bucket list" is starting to look like:

~~Should~~

~~Would~~

~~Could~~

DID √

Write down your dreams. Don't get discouraged. Dreams don't have deadlines. Make a long list of things you want to have in your life.

Dream big.

There is only one person that can dream your dreams and live your life — and you see her in the mirror every day.

wear your life well

share your story

I'm not interested in being perfect when I am older. I'm interested in having a narrative. It's the narrative that's really the most beautiful thing about women.

~Jodie Foster

Talking with women across the country over the years has highlighted for me that our life journey is not a one-size-fits-all trip. We all have unique stories that share a common thread. Diverse women ranging in age from 18 to 87 have divulged a desire we all share: to love ourselves and to improve the quality of our lives.

As have I, these women have all had welcome highs and difficult lows. Life gave them these twists and turns too. I listened to them as they shared their dreams — dreams they left behind, dreams they want to re-kindle and dreams they have yet to uncover. Some women were feeling stuck and standing at cross-roads in their lives. Others were living amazing and inspiring lives because they overcame their fears and found new ways to their next happy.

I have heard stories that changed my life and, in hindsight, realized that they were very specific to what I needed to hear at the time. The impact stories have on us is personal. They help us to see things from a new perspective just when we need it. Iyanla Vanzant reminds us that "it's important that we share experiences with other people. Your story will heal you and your story will heal someone else. When you tell your story, you free yourself and give other people permission to acknowledge their own story."

What I have come to understand is that small stories often go untold, yet, we all struggle with the same basic fears and insecurities. The most common is the feeling that we are not enough. That unhealthy belief is so powerful that sometimes it sabotages us from going after what we truly want to experience in life.

And I thought it was just me.

I have made many changes in my life. I've discovered that the power to design a life I love is already in me, no matter what the situation. As the author of my life it is in my power to make my story great. If I don't like how the plot is developing I start to take it in new directions. I get to write the ending. Author Anais Nin spoke a summation that resonates with me when she said "I take pleasure in my transformations. I look quiet and consistent but few know how many women there are in me."

In telling you my stories I have been open. I have left myself exposed and vulnerable. I have given myself permission to be both scared and brave in sharing my past and present struggles with you.

It has been an honor taking my journey of self-reflection and life lessons with you. I hope my sharing has reminded you that you are more wonderful, more beautiful, more capable and more loveable than you imagine.

Engage in your life *right now* and find the magic in your story. Embrace energetically the next changes and find the beauty in the new opportunities that life will gift you.

I leave you with a wonderful thought: Some of the best days of our lives haven't happened yet.

lessons from the journey

forgive yourself

find your voice

make a difference

cherish your mother

embrace your evolution

get playful

find your funny

get over getting older

be your own hero

grow through life

never give up

look for the treasures in life's scars

live like there's no tomorrow

share your story

Download bonus *wear your life well* content at
www.wearyourlifewell.com

wear your life well

off the cuff

to be honest,

i'm just trying to figure it out as I go.

my life. my outfits.

everything.

to be continued ...

wear your life well

my manifesto

design your life get into change shape. express your essence. find your groove. decide your destiny. start where you are. believe that good things are on their way. forget about being perfect. mind your thoughts. believe in day dreams. knock on the door. do it for you. say YES to being a rock star. reinvent yourself. find joy on the journey. *fashion your style* make room for a new you. recognize your value. claim your confidence. stay true to yourself. learn to say no. reveal your true colors. live a colorful life. walk on the wild side. love what you've got. treat yourself gently. don't label yourself. search for something new. uncover your secret strength. know you are deserving. *love your life* forgive yourself. find your voice. make a difference. cherish your mother. embrace your evolution. get playful. find your funny. get over getting older. be your own hero. grow through life. never give up. look for the treasures in life's scars. live like there is no tomorrow. share your story. *wear your life well*

wear your life well

acknowledgements

For years I have known that I wanted to influence women, to help them reach their awe-inspiring capacity to be amazing and change the world. When I decided to write *Wear Your Life Well* I wasn't *exactly* sure what it would be about. I "just knew" I needed to do it. As I began putting words on pages suddenly this book started writing me.

It takes a village. Some may call it a tribe. I could not bring this book to the world without the extraordinary people in my life who, every day, remind me of my essential purpose and challenge me to become the best version of myself. They have been a part of my past and they help me to create my present and future. I am humbled by their belief in me. Thank you.

To my editor, Lynne Rach. You are so much more than a wordsmith. Thank you for your faith in me and for your friendship. You trusted my vision and never hesitated to give of your precious time and talent to make this book better. With your uncanny combination of strength and gentleness you coached me, challenged me, encouraged me and helped me to bring my words to life.

To my graphic design goddess Jacquie Morris who, for many years, has made my passions come alive visually. Thank you, dear friend, for your assistance and all-around awesomeness.

To my family. You are my biggest motivation and I feel your love. We have always been there for each other, in good times and in bad, and we always will be. My mother Elise, you have been a pivotal role model in my life and that is where this memoir begins. My children Chris and Lisa, I love you and cherish you. My grandchildren Zoë and Coen, you make my heart happy and inspire me to want to make the world a better place for the generations to come.

To my friends. You are strong, caring, independent, creative, opinionated, kind, unique and truly inspirational women. A big thank you to the women in my circle who enrich my life and are helping to shine light on women's advancement.

And to Scottie, for your patience, your support and your belief in me. I love you. Für evich.

about the author

Helene Oseen is an ambassador for women. Her passion and mission is to inspire women to love who they are, to own their power and to create their best life.

She encourages women on their life-long journey to learn, transform and expand life's experiences in pursuit of happiness — and that perfect outfit. As a style expert, speaker and author she dispenses both wisdom and wardrobe advice in her always *true-to-the-female-experience* way.

She is still young enough to enjoy fashion, old enough to have

seen the trends before, real enough to embrace her stage in life and friendly enough to keep it fun.

Helene strives to stay true to herself in her ongoing discovery of who she is and what can be. She lives with her husband Scottie (who makes her laugh) in Calgary, Alberta.

Helene is a distinguished recipient of the Global Woman of Vision Award. Honoring exceptional women, it is bestowed on leaders who have implemented their passion and whose personal dedication and actions inspire others to new levels of success.

my gift to you

your journey through journaling

Are you ready for some self-exploration? That's what writing *Wear Your Life Well: Lessons on the Journey to your Truest Self* was about for me. I didn't just write these stories. I lived them.

Because we are women, our stories intertwine, and yet, each of our stories are as unique as our thumbprint. Life isn't a one-size-fits-all adventure.

I am committed to helping you find your truest self. That is why I composed a companion book *Wear Your Life Well: Your Journey through Journaling*. It is filled with pro-active tools to spark reflection through thoughtful writing, drawing, scribbles, doodles personal exploration and more.

The activities act as a call-to guide to jump-start your journey and by doing them you will find answers to the questions that help you gain a deeper understanding of who you are, what you want and the meaning of your life.

Every answer is inside you.

Download your copy today
www.wearyourlifewell.com

please review this book

Thank you for reading *Wear your Life Well*. Within these pages are stories of my life and the gems of insight and inspiration I gleaned as the moral of each defining moment. I hope they resonate and lead you to understand that you are not alone in trying to navigate (the good, the bad, the insane and the awkward) real-life ups and downs.

I hope this collection of my memories and musing as well as my secrets to savvy style, delighted you. If they did, I'd be grateful if you would take a few minutes to write a review on Amazon and give my book as many stars as you think it deserves.

Thank you in advance. I appreciate your help spreading the word.

www.amazon.com/author/heleneoseen

let's be friends

Join our on-line community of women and tap into the collective wisdom of girlfriends.

It's an e-gathering place to explore everything that matters to you. Whatever part of your life needs tweaking you'll get the insights and motivation you need to live your life with more spirit, sass and style.

Questions? Want some advice? Ready to rant? Give us your opinions, share your insights and join in the conversation. Let's laugh, cope and give each other hope.

facebook.com/heleneoseenwearyourlifewell

instagram.com@heleneoseen

LIFE
makeover
inside
+OUT

~~New~~ You.
TRUE You.

**simple strategies to
add more smile and style
into your life**

wear your life well

visit

www.wearyourlifewell.com

www.heleneoseen.com